Advance Praise for *Radical Relevance*

"I think Cates' concept of the 'Right-Fit Client' is spot on. Not only does Cates make the case for why we need to continually narrow our focus, he shows us how to do it. I found his chapter on the neuroscience of relevance both fascinating and practical."

—Verne Harnish
Founder, Entrepreneurs' Organization (EO), and author of *Scaling Up (Rockefeller Habits 2.0)*

"We've been working with Bill Cates for years, using his strategies and methods to attract more ideal clients. In *Radical Relevance*, Cates challenges us to communicate our value in a way that is instantly meaningful to our prospects and clients."

—Dean R. Thibault
Executive Vice President-Commercial Banking, Landmark National Bank

"What Cates, a long-time icon in the field of referral-based sales and marketing, has done in this magnificent work is nothing less than provide the ultimate sales success road map. If you're a leader/manager, be sure each and every member of your team has this book; go through it together chapter by chapter. WOW—fantastic!"

—Bob Burg
Coauthor of *The Go-Giver* Series

"If you ignore the perspectives in this book, you run the risk of being ignored in the marketplace. What makes *Radical Relevance* a compelling read is that it's based on strategies and tactics that real businesses are using to grow in just the right direction. My company has been implementing Cates' concepts for years—to great results. This may be his best work yet."

—Bruce Davison, CFP
President / CEO, Strategic Financial Concepts, Inc.

"Cates' strength as a communicator is the ability to deconstruct a topic into logical components, and then create practical steps to effect change. If you want actionable ideas that will produce results, this book is for you."

—Michael Schmidtmann
CEO, Trans4mers, LLC

"Bill Cates has done it again! *Radical Relevance* shows you the cutting-edge strategies, tactics, and tools to win more business right now. We live in a hyper-connected, super-noisy, always-on marketing and sales world. Follow Bill's advice on connection, relationship, relevance, and value. Implement everything in these pages, and you'll produce remarkable results."

—David Newman, CSP
Author of *Do It! Marketing* and *Do It! Speaking*

"Understanding the significance and incorporating 'relevance' is the foundation for any successful professional seeking to build a meaningful business through referrals. Bill provides you the exercises, processes, and action steps necessary to incorporate these essentials skills."

—William Wright, CFP
Entrepreneur, Influencer, Speaker, and Founder/CEO,
Financial Professionals Group

Radical RELEVANCE

SHARPEN YOUR MARKETING MESSAGE
CUT THROUGH THE NOISE
WIN MORE IDEAL CLIENTS

BILL CATES

Thunder Hill Press
705 Childs Point Road
Suite 102
Annapolis, MD 21401
Printed in the United States of America
First Edition: September 2019
1 2 3 4 5 6 7 8 9 10
Library of Congress Control Number: 2019912691
ISBN - 978-1-888970-01-2 (hardcover)
ISBN - 978-1-888970-02-9 (paperback)

1. Business 2. Marketing 3. Sales 4. Professional Services 5. Small Business
Book Design by Sheila Parr
Edited by Sandra Beckwith

This book is dedicated to my fiancée Laura, who has encouraged me to "finish the damn book" and has had the kindness and decency to not remind me that she's way out of my league. Joking aside, she has been incredibly supportive in all aspects of my business.

CONTENTS

The Buyer's Lament

Don't waste my time, please go away.
I will not talk with you today.
You call me up, you want to sell.
But all you do is tell, tell, tell.

I do not want to hear your spiel.
I will not play let's make a deal.
So listen up, take my advice.
Discover how you can entice.

If you aspire to earn my trust,
Research is an absolute must.
Know my goals, the issues I face.
Use them to build your business case.

What have you done for firms like mine?
How have you helped their bottom line?
Can you cut my costs or help me grow?
Now that's the info I want to know.

If you can help me solve my plight,
I'm wide open to your fresh insight.
I always look for new perspectives
So I can reach my big objectives.

If you want me to remember your name,
Launch an account entry campaign.
When big opportunities are at stake,
Ten or more contacts is what it may take.

To get yourself past my no-entry zone,
Think of this before you email or phone.
Once you get your foot in the door,
I guarantee you'll sell lots more!

Jill Konrath
Sales Poet & Author
www.JillKonrath.com

REGISTER THIS BOOK FOR FREE RESOURCES

Get Instant Access to the Radical Relevance Toolkit*

When you go to www.RadicalRelevanceToolkit.com, you'll find a treasure trove of resources—all designed to help you acquire more Right-Fit Clients™.

Here's a sample of the resources you'll find:

- The Radical Relevance Action Guide
- Creating Your Radically Relevant and Compelling Website
- Creating Your Right-Fit Client™ Personas
- Your Relevant and Compelling Email Messaging Guide
- Creating Your Magnetic LinkedIn Profile

* We add new resources continuously. As a registered owner of this book, you will receive occasional updates alerting you we've added new tools to help you grow your business.

To register, go to: www.RadicalRelevanceToolkit.com

FOREWORD

Radical Relevance Begins with a Total Shift in Mindset

I think Bill Cates has nailed it with his concept of *radical relevance*. Your value proposition must be relevant to your prospects or they won't give you the time of day. In addition, if you don't continue to be relevant to your customers, they'll leave you as soon as someone more relevant comes along.

It's not your prospects' job to figure out your value to them. It's *your* job to develop and communicate your value in a way that will resonate with your ideal clients.

Relevance is in the eye of the beholder. Relevance is understanding how your prospects and customers interpret your value for themselves.

Relevance requires awareness of:

1. Your understanding of who you are and who you want to attract.
2. Your ability to see yourself through the eyes of prospects and customers.

When I became president of High Point University in 2005, it was a fine school that provided a good education. But there was an air of complacency. HPU was on the verge of becoming irrelevant.

Being charged with guiding this institution into the future, I knew that we could no longer settle for "fine." I had a vision to turn HPU into a nationally prominent private university. I knew that it would take all the knowledge, skills, and experience I had accumulated from 35 years in the business world as an entrepreneur and corporate board member.

It was hard work, and we're still not finished. But we have undergone a remarkable transformation that has nearly tripled undergraduate enrollment, size of the faculty, and added five academic schools.

U.S. News & World Report ranked HPU as both the #1 Regional College in the South and the #1 for the most innovative school. In 2017, *Princeton Review* rated us in the top 20 of its Best-Run Colleges.

We did this by being relevant to prospective students, their parents, and our faculty.

Relevance is Empathy in Action

I agree with Bill when he says that *empathy* is one of the most powerful tools in sales and marketing. A message that demonstrates that we understand our prospects' and customers' challenges, opportunities, fears, and dreams will be a message that resonates instantly with them. We want to stop them in their tracks and make them think, "This is a message worthy of my time and attention."

Staying focused on relevance is how High Point University grew from a small, comfortable academic institution into an admired institution of higher learning. It's how we continue to offer relevant and compelling value to our university community.

Read *Radical Relevance* from cover to cover. And implement the ideas as you go. After all, ideas are worthless without action.

Nido Qubein
President, High Point University
(www.HighPoint.edu)

PREFACE

The Timeless Ingredient in Every Thriving Business

Have you heard the amusing statement, "Just when I found all the answers, they changed all the questions?" That pretty much sums up how I came to write this book.

Since 1995, I've been writing, speaking, and consulting on business growth through referrals and introductions. I've written four books on the topic, spoken to hundreds of thousands of professionals and business owners around the world, and consulted for companies of all sizes. I've done all of this with the intention of helping them increase their revenue without adding to their marketing budgets.

After my first book, *Unlimited Referrals,* was released, many organizations hired me to speak, train, and consult on how to ask for referrals without pushing (still one of my most popular sessions). They liked the process I created and the scripts I provided because they worked.

I don't trust you enough to give you referrals.

As I taught businesses how to be proactive for referrals, I discovered that many of the folks weren't *referable* in the first place. They had little or no success asking for referrals and introductions because the people they were asking did not see enough value or trust them to handle the referral appropriately. It didn't take me long to realize that I needed to help individuals and businesses develop a client journey that created more client engagement in two main areas—the value connection and the human (or personal) connection.

What do you say to your prospects?

Later, as preparation for a speech, I was interviewing some of the more successful financial professionals in the company that hired me. I asked each of them, "What do you say to your new referral prospects when reaching out to them?"

I was astonished to hear their weak approaches. Many had no set process and most just made non-compelling statements such as, "I'd like to get together to tell you about the work I do." (Like anyone has time for that?)

Having taught my referral processes for more than 24 years, I can tell you with great confidence that these reps had gained a decent level of success even though they didn't express a compelling value.

This experience made me realize two things:

1. The strength of an introduction from a trusted source will compensate for a weak way of expressing your value, but it will only take you so far.
2. I needed to write this book to help my clients develop and communicate more relevant and compelling value so they attract and sustain their prospects' interest and move them to action.

Here's the foundation for your business success.

One thing I know for sure: Reaching qualified prospects for your business is unlikely to get any easier for you unless you are willing to take a fresh look at your value proposition and how you communicate your value.

Your value proposition isn't just the words you use or the look of your website. Your value proposition is the totality of how you show up in your business. Even the subtlest of things work to communicate your value. The goal, of course, is to keep all of this as congruent as possible. Otherwise, you run the risk of confusing prospects and clients. As Donald Miller (*Building Your Story Brand*) said, "If you confuse, you lose."

Your ability to develop, believe in, and communicate your value is foundational to your business success.

Your guide to abundant growth and profitability.

I hope you will allow me to be your guide as you build your business based on a solid foundation of real value that will help you achieve the level of financial freedom you've always wanted.

INTRODUCTION

Are you winning the race for relevance? My goal with this book is to help you understand and overcome two looming challenges.

Challenge #1: Marketing Message Overload

We live in a world of marketing message overload. It's been estimated that the average person is exposed to approximately 3,000 marketing messages every 24 hours. If you average seven hours of sleep per day, that's 176 marketing messages per waking hour or three marketing messages every minute.

One of your brain's primary purposes is to help you navigate your environment in a meaningful way. Your brain is dedicated to action. Another one of its main jobs is to keep you alive by helping to conserve energy by reducing the number of calories (energy) you expend each day. Because processing these messages takes energy, the message bombardment isn't healthy for your body, being, or business.

By design, your brain has to sift through all the stimuli coming at you about six times per second (that's fast), assessing, "Am I safe? Is that a threat?"

Safe? Threat? Safe? Threat? Along with that are: Relevant? Irrelevant? Pay attention? Ignore?

Once the brain feels safe, it moves on to looking for opportunities, novelty, anything interesting. (Don't you wish you could just turn your brain off for a few minutes?)

Without this critical and discerning part of our brains, we'd go nuts, crazy, bonkers, and batty. (I'll cover this in more depth in Chapter 3: The Neuroscience of Relevance.)

This is why human beings crave relevance and clarity! Communicate to others with clarity and relevance and they'll listen to you. Communicate irrelevant or confusing messages and they will ignore you. If ever there was a time for us to think in terms of radical relevance, it's now.

The only way for your business to compete in this world of marketing-message overload is to find ways to be *super relevant to just the right prospects*. You want your messaging to hit the bullseye in your ideal clients' brains so it creates immediate and ongoing resonance with them.

Imagine one of those dramatic, love-at-first-sight scenes in the movies. You know, the ones where people lock eyes from across the room, they move toward each other (in slow motion, of course), and everyone else in the room falls into soft focus. Cue the music, hearts, and doves. Radical relevance is the business equivalent of love at first sight.

This message overload has created barriers to creating love at first sight for your prospects. It's becoming harder and harder to cut through all the noise and grab someone's attention so that they'll stop for two seconds to see if what you are saying is of any value to them.

What's the solution? Relevance! *Radical relevance!*

Challenge #2: Inertia

After cutting through all the barriers to get someone's attention, the next challenge we face is getting them to take action. You'll hear me say this a few times throughout this book: You have to be *radically relevant* to cut through the barriers and grab someone's attention, and you have to be *critically compelling* to get them moving and keep them moving.

One dictionary definition of the word compel says, "To force or drive, especially to a course of action." To my mind, compel means movement or action. No force allowed!

If I had to say which should come first—being relevant or being compelling—I'd have to say relevant because you can't move someone to action if they don't know about you. With that said, the compelling part of your message needs to occur at either the same time or almost immediately after to keep the process going. If your message ever stops being relevant or if you aren't moving them to act, you've lost them.

With that in mind, this book is structured so that it's in line with how I approach the content that I deliver through speeches, consulting, coaching, and online video training programs.

PART 1 discusses the principles and science behind radical relevance. Both need to be understood before you can develop strategies that will help you accomplish sales goals. Think of PART 1 as laying the groundwork for the rest of the book.

PART 2 focuses on the strategies you need to consider and put in place before getting tactical. Engaging in tactics before making sure you have the right strategy in place will mean that you waste resources.

In PARTS 3 and 4 we get very tactical. You don't want to go there, though, until you're following the right principles and strategies.

This book is designed to help you become radically relevant to your prospects and clients. The net result to you will be more impact, influence, and—yes—income.

PART 1

Why You Must Be Radically Relevant

As humans, we are always seeking to be relevant—to our families, jobs, communities, and even to ourselves. Heck, a life without relevance can be depressingly empty.

In the business world, relevance is everything. Either you're continually relevant or you risk being completely ignored.

Google, Amazon, and YouTube are the ultimate relevance machines. Commodities such as bottled water, toothpaste, and breakfast cereals are creating multiple versions in their attempt to attract the right buyer with the right product.

Of course, trying to be relevant to your audience is nothing new. Every experienced marketer or copywriter understands the importance of saying the right thing to the right person in the right way at the right time.

From a business development standpoint, the shortest path to relevance with a new prospect is an introduction from someone that prospect already trusts. This is one reason I've devoted one quarter of my life to helping professionals and businesses go from incremental to exponential growth using the combined power of purposeful word of mouth, recommendations, referrals, and introductions from advocates.

Before you can do that, you need to understand radical relevance and what it means to your success. Part 1 will help with that.

900 Percent Growth

I've got something of a "footnote" for you, though, before you immerse yourself in what's to follow. I know that you might be saying to yourself, "I hope this book is worth the read. I'm not really interested in a bunch of theory with no proven track record."

So I have a question for you. How would you like to go from 100 to 1,000 high-value clients in seven years?

One of my clients who has used the strategies in this book has done exactly that. Nancy MacKay, founder of MacKay CEO Forums (www.MacKayCEOForums.com), has built an extremely successful enterprise that brings CEOs of privately held businesses together in forum groups where they help each other solve their biggest challenges.

In her first five years, Nancy built her company up to 100 members. Her business was thriving, and her CEO clients loved the experience and results. Nancy wanted more, though. She wanted to scale her business; she wanted to go from incremental to exponential growth.

When she contacted me to help accelerate her business growth, I could tell immediately that she was smart, hardworking, and driven. I knew I was working with someone who truly believed in the value she brought to clients, was a sponge for new ideas, and was someone who would actually implement those ideas. For a business-growth consultant, that's the perfect storm!

I'm proud to say that at the time of this writing, using the concepts, strategies, and methods put forth in this book (and my other books), MacKay CEO Forums has grown 900 percent in seven years—from 100 CEO members to 1,000. I don't know about you, but I'd call that exponential growth.

In a recent conversation with Nancy, she told me that our initial conversations were "a real game-changer." And let's give credit where credit is due. Yes, I provided ideas, guidance, and even specific word tracks to Nancy and her team. But she did the work! She applied the ideas in a way that produced these outstanding results.

Initially, we worked on creating a culture of referrals for MacKay CEO Forums with such things as:

1. Installing a specific process for approaching CEO members for introductions to prospective members.
2. Adapting that same process to generate introductions to new forum chairs who could build and run their own forums.
3. Providing video-based training and telephone coaching to all MacKay CEO Forums staff and Forums chairs.
4. Brainstorming rewards programs for referrals—for both the members and the chairs.

More recently, we've been working together on the many concepts and strategies outlined in this book. I want to show you how MacKay CEO Forums has addressed each concept, so I'm sharing that in a tool at the end of this book in the Appendix. There, you'll find "The Radical Relevance Value Gap Assessment." After each question in the assessment, you'll see how MacKay has implemented some of this book's strategies. As you complete that assessment after you read the book, that company's experience will help you envision how you can adopt and adapt the concepts and assessment for your specific situation.

Now, let's get started with making your business radically relevant.

CHAPTER 1

The Rules of Radical Relevance

Radical relevance is about finding the bullseye for your business. You start with a relentless passion for truly knowing your clients so you can identify and solve their critical challenges and maximize their opportunities. You narrow your focus to define a clear and profitable target market. Then you further narrow your focus to identify your Right-Fit Clients™.

This ever-increasing narrowing of your focus allows you to sharpen your marketing message—to cut through all the noise in the marketplace, resonate with your prospects to capture their attention, and compel them to take action.

Radical relevance is about solving the right problems with the right product or service, for the right people, with the right message, through the right medium, at just the right time. Radical relevance is not a theory. Radical relevance is a blueprint for more effective action that leads to the growth of your business.

What is a Right-Fit Client™? Your Right-Fit Clients are those you are meant to serve. They are right for you because you are right for them and vice versa. Right-fit prospects will resonate immediately with your message. Right-fit prospects will say to themselves, "Finally! Someone who gets me!"

Right-Fit Clients are typically a joy to work with. They are also more profitable. Your processes are geared to serve these types of clients, and they appreciate your value for all the reasons you want them to.

Your Right-Fit Client is like your business soul mate!

The 17 Rules of Radical Relevance

Before we take a deep dive into the principles, strategies, and tactics associated with radical relevance, here are a few "rules" for you to consider. They will help you evaluate how you are applying this concept of radical relevance to your business.

1. **The shortest route to relevance is through an introduction from a trusted source.** Referrals and Introductions work because of borrowed trust. When a trusted source makes a solid introduction, you are automatically relevant.
2. **Give your clients a seat at the table.** Never develop services, product offers, or marketing messages without speaking to some of your clients. This is how you guarantee relevance.
3. **Value is in the eye of the beholder.** It's your job to determine, develop, and communicate your value in a way that will resonate with the prospects who are a perfect fit for your business.
4. **Meet your prospects where they are.** Before talking about the journey of transformation you will create for your clients, find out where they are in that journey. Everyone who comes to you will be at a different place—their place.
5. **Only differences that matter, matter.** Why is your differentiation important and/or valuable to your clients? What is the benefit that your distinction brings to your clients?
6. **Differentiation for differentiation sake is worthless.** The goal

of creating differentiation is to create both perceived and real value to your prospects and clients.

7. **Market to people.** An industry and a company are made up of people. Market to the people in that industry and company.
8. **Think solutions and benefits before promotion.** Before you promote your solutions, first focus on the transformation your offer creates for your clients. Spend 70 percent discussing the transformation and 30 percent on how you'll make that happen.
9. **Relevance begins with client obsession.** Radical relevance starts with your obsession for knowing your prospects and clients better than you previously thought necessary and certainly more than your competition does.
10. **Differentiate between your different "personas."** A "persona" is your ideal client profile. Segment your marketing message based on the personas you've identified rather than on your products/services. Apply the right products/services based on which persona you are addressing.
11. **Know your own client focused "why."** Why do you believe in your value? What experiences or shifts in perspectives have you seen that cause you to believe you can bring great value to your clients?
12. **Know your persona's "why."** What motivated them to meet with you? What are the critical problems and/or most coveted opportunities in their life? What motivates them to take action?
13. **Use more personal messaging.** Go from impersonal (therefore less relevant) messaging—using words such as *we*, *our*, *they*, and *their*—to more personal messaging (relevant) by using words such as *you* and *your*.
14. **Your prospects and clients demand relevance.** Be relevant or be ignored. Be compelling or be forgotten.
15. **Your prospects and clients aren't mind readers.** Never assume a prospect or client can read your mind and take the action you

desire. If you want them to do something, ask them to do it. Use a call to action.

16. **Test, test, test.** This is a universal rule of marketing. You can make certain assumptions based on your own experience and/or intuition, and what other experts suggest, but you'll never know for certain until you test your ideas.
17. **Resist the urge to expand your target.** The tendency for most is to widen their target to be more inclusive. Resist this. The more inclusive your messaging, the less impactful and effective it will be.

The Benefits of Focusing on Relevance

Remaining relevant to your prospects and clients—and communicating your relevance in a clear way—is foundational to your business success.

Here are a few of the many benefits of keeping the concept of relevance top of mind whenever you think about communicating your value. A more relevant message will:

- Grab your prospects' attention and stimulate their interest.
- Build trust more quickly.
- Present more actionable solutions to your prospects and clients.
- Increase decision-making speed.
- Be more likely to turn into action.
- But that's not all. Relevance also:
- Yields processes, products, and services that bring more value.
- Focuses your marketing time and dollars more efficiently.
- Makes your marketing more effective so it yields better results.
- Creates more effective prospecting efforts that yield better results.
- Gives you confidence because you know your efforts are appropriate and on target.

You and I live in a world that demands radical relevance. To ignore this important perspective is to be ignored in the marketplace.

RADICALLY RELEVANT ACTION STEPS

1. Go through the "17 Rules of Radical Relevance" again, more slowly. What rules are you already following?
2. What rules do you need to apply to your messaging?

"Your radically relevant message will be irresistible to just the right prospects, compelling them to follow your recommendations, while simultaneously repelling those prospects who aren't a perfect fit for your business."

—Bill Cates

RADICAL RULE OF RELEVANCE #1

The shortest route to relevance is through an introduction from a trusted source. Referrals and Introductions work because of borrowed trust. When a trusted source makes a solid introduction, you are automatically relevant.

CHAPTER 2

Be Relevant or Be Ignored

In his book, *Principles: Life and Work*, Ray Dalio writes, "Recognize that to gain the perspective that comes from seeing things through another's eyes, you must suspend judgment for a time—only by empathizing can you properly evaluate another point of view."

This is a big ask from Dalio. He wants us to set aside our biases about how we believe our product or service best suits the person we're attempting to influence. Easier said than done.

However, seeing the world through the eyes of your prospects and clients is at the heart of relevance. You have to learn enough about the other person's logistical and emotional context before you stand a shot at earning the right to their attention and compelling them to take action.

When my current business was focused on helping professionals and businesses acquire more clients through referrals and introductions, I saw the world through the glasses of engagement and leverage. I was always thinking, "How do I help my clients become more referable with *their* clients so they earn the right to referrals and introductions?" And, "How do I help my clients convert the value they have provided and the goodwill they have established into introductions to new clients and other potential advocates?"

With my new focus on helping businesses create more relevant and compelling client-attraction messages, I see the world through a new pair of glasses. I notice how my clients (and other marketers) are being effective with their relevant and compelling messages. And I notice when they're not.

Actually, I should probably say that I'm wearing bifocals. Half of the lens is seeing the world in terms of *engagement* and *leverage,* and the other half is seeing *relevant* and *compelling.* I can't wait for my next book. Trifocals, here I come.

The Race for Relevance

Are you positioned to win the race for relevance? Did you even know that there was a race for relevance? Allow me to explain.

Let's say you're about to start an internet search. You pull up Google and begin to type your search term. You're two or three words into it, and Google has read your mind—the rest of your search words magically appear. It's uncanny. Even scary at times. Clearly, search engines depend on their ability to be relevant.

Look at Amazon and other online shopping sites. As you search for an item, the site suggests other, relevant items you might consider. They say, "People who have purchased this have also purchased that."

Admit it. You love it! Assuming you don't get overwhelmed with choices, you find exactly what you were searching for and a whole lot more. You place the order.

And then there's YouTube. I can tell a lot about a person just by looking at their computer screen while they're on YouTube and observing the other videos it recommends for that specific viewer.

Relevance is fundamental. Radical relevance has become ubiquitous.

Commodities Have Entered the Race

When was the last time you shopped for toothpaste? Have you seen the selection these days? With whitening—without whitening. Tartar control—no tartar control. Minty fresh? Enamel protecting? Organic?

And what about bottled water? With fizz, without fizz. With flavor, without flavor. With sugar, with artificial sweetener, with Stevia. With vitamins, without vitamins. Smart water, dumb water? Do we really need all those choices?

Here's the deal. If commodities like water and toothpaste go to great lengths to be super relevant for their customers, what makes any professional or business think they can thrive by not attending to this critical aspect of their business?

We Live in a Radically Relevant World

Marketers within a wide variety of industries (and even political campaigns) have discovered the power of *microtargeting* (also called micro-niche targeting). This strategy uses consumer data and demographics to identify the interests of individuals or small groups of like-minded individuals.

In addition to helping a marketer choose the right communication channel, microtargeting can help dictate the exact words you should use to attract a prospect's attention and move them to take action. We see this clearly in presidential campaigns, when staffers collect and update individual voter data, then apply predictive analytics. This strategy helps campaigns direct specific messages to specific people.

Big Data Creates the Possibility for Radical Relevance

In *Buyer Personas*, Adele Revella (www.BuyerPersona.com) writes, "The collection of massive quantities of data about nearly every living person on the planet is ushering in marketing's new frontier. The anonymous demographic information revealed in consumer surveys of the recent past is paltry compared to the myriad intelligence currently in the hands of commercial data brokers. The practice of onboarding—the merging of data collected from multiple sites with specific identifying information—has created detailed, individual digital marketing dossiers."

Scary? Yup! "They" know where we are, what we're doing, and how we feel. Heck, I don't even know that about myself half the time.

Another example of radical relevance is the proliferation of fun, clever, and productive apps for our smartphones. If your mind imagines an app that could make your life easier, somebody has probably already developed it. By their nature, most apps are radically relevant.

Electronic billboards are another example. The billboard industry now collects data from driver GPS apps. This data tells them when certain categories of people are driving in any given area, thus allowing the electronic billboard to display advertisements most relevant to that demographic.

Some billboards are even equipped with pollen sensors so when the pollen count is up, the billboard displays allergy medicine advertisements.

A Double-Edged Sword

The explosion of new technology has made it easier and less costly to reach people with your message (at least in theory). But since these tools are so easy to use, message bombardment is only increasing. Everywhere we look there's a message that says, "Pay attention to me!"

If we don't become—and remain—radically relevant and critically compelling, we will fall further and further back in the pack and run the risk of going the way of Kodak, Borders Books, Blockbuster, and Napster, to name just a few.

Radical Relevance Is About Narrowing Your Focus

The Digital Marketing 4FP website (https://digitalmarketing4fp.com) lists how digital marketing can help you narrow your focus and create more relevant messaging for just the right people. Here's my slightly adjusted version of that list.

- *Personas*: Getting perfectly clear on your ideal client profile—who you want to attract, where you find them, and the right time to offer your solutions.
- *Client journey*: Creating strategies for how these perfect prospects can move from having never heard of you, to evaluating your firm, to coming on board, and even becoming a great source for referrals.
- *Content marketing*: Developing just the right content that prospects can find in just the right places (blogging, podcasts, webinars, articles) to attract the right prospects and repel the wrong ones.
- *Email marketing*: Creating subject lines and messages that attract and keep the prospect's attention and deliver a compelling reason for the action you request.
- *Search engine optimization—SEO marketing*: Employing search terms and phrases your ideal prospects are searching for so your website or LinkedIn profile shows up on the first page of search results.

Radical relevance should play a role in all your sales and marketing—digital or otherwise. We will examine these concepts in more depth throughout the course of this book.

THE MAGICAL POWERS OF A RIGHT-FIT MARKET

When I started working with Jayson Lowe, cofounder of Ascendant Financial in Canada and coauthor of *The Bankers' Secret, A Simple Guide to Creating Personal Wealth for Canadians*, he had already built a successful financial advisory business. We focused on developing his value proposition for a new target market—physicians and dentists.

He began to see a difference after connecting with an accountant who also targeted dentists. After Jayson shared his full process and the unique value he brought to these medical professionals, the accounting firm began hosting dinners that would allow them to introduce their clients to Jayson.

This is one of the magical benefits of zeroing in on a specific target market. You can partner with others serving that market in a way that helps everyone—including the clients.

What does it cost Jayson to get in front of these highly qualified prospects by way of endorsement from a highly trusted source? Let me grab my calculator. Hmm . . . zero dollars! (And you didn't believe me when I said you can boost your revenue without increasing your marketing budget.)

May I Tell You a Quick Story?

Yes? Thank you. A number of years ago, I started a specialty book publishing company. My first book was a strawberry cookbook that I sold to pick-your-own strawberry farms across the U.S. Annual sales quickly averaged about 20,000 books.

Because the strawberry-selling season is so short in most states, I decided to publish an apple cookbook. Much longer selling season! I sold that book to apple orchards with roadside stands and pick-your-own farms. I quickly learned that apple growers use bees to pollinate the apple blossoms. So my next book? A honey cookbook.

I was selling the *right book* to the *right customer* in the *right place*, with the *right offer*, at the *right time*. That's relevance that hits the bullseye.

The Rest of the Story

Selling 80,000 to 100,000 books per year was good, but I wanted more. I decided to go after manufacturers of cooking equipment and appliances to help them produce cookbooks to package with their equipment. While I had some success in this new niche, business was . . . forgive the pun . . . a slow cooker.

Then, I had a rare moment of clarity bordering on brilliance. Until this point, my company's name was WRC Publishing—William Richard Cates—and was meaningless outside my family. I changed the name to The American Cooking Guild, and the game changed for me almost overnight. I mean . . . who would *you* buy a cookbook from? WRC Publishing or The American Cooking Guild?

In 1983, one of my publishing company's authors appeared on the Baltimore TV show "People Are Talking" hosted by Richard Sher and a young, up-and-coming talent by the name of Oprah Winfrey. (Ever heard of her?) The book was cleverly titled *Hooked on Seafood.*

Several months later, an executive with Bumble Bee Seafoods, the largest manufacturer of canned tuna in North America, approached me about purchasing a large quantity of *Hooked on Seafood* to use as a premium in grocery stores to help sell more canned tuna and salmon. The company purchased 400,000 copies.

That sale changed my life.

First, the author received a great royalty check. Second, as the sales rep, I got a pretty large commission. Third, I was the company owner and got all the rest. I eventually sold that business in 1989 and believe it has been sold several times since.

Figure 1

This illustrates some of the key principles of radical relevance: the right product, for the right market, at the right time.

The 8 Principles of Radical Relevance

Fundamental to your success in any marketing or sales effort are seven principles that I urge you to always keep in mind. Skip any one of these steps only after careful consideration.

- Target the *right market*
- Target the *right person* (the bullseye)
- Solve the *right problems* (and opportunities)
- Deliver the *right product/service*
- Make the *right offer*
- Use the *right medium*
- Execute the *right timing*
- Employ the *right messaging*

As I introduce you to each of these guiding principles, I'd like to begin with a story that you might find interesting. Then, I'll go into a bit of detail about each of them.

"Dollars in Your Mailbox"

My education in radical relevance started in 1978 when I came across a magazine ad with the headline, "How to Get Big Dollars in Your Mailbox—Every Day." The long-copy ad, an advertorial, was compelling enough for me to order the book being advertised—Ernest P. Weckesser's *Dollars in Your Mailbox: The Beginner's Guide to Selling Information By Mail.*

How's that for a title? Who wouldn't want dollars in their mailbox?

Because I was in a dead-end job (my *problem*) and wanted to earn more (my *opportunity*), that book title was immediately *relevant* to me. I didn't have to think about it. It was automatic. I wanted to make more money, so the ad *compelled* me to purchase and read the book, then apply the principles. I literally immersed myself in the world of direct-response marketing.

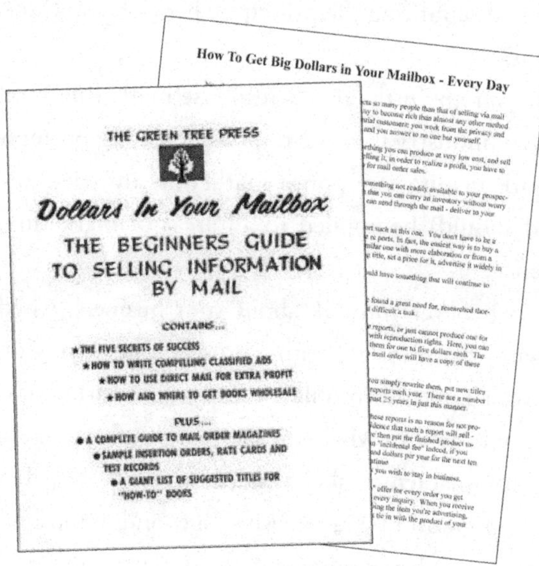

Figure 2

I have made millions of dollars following the principles of direct response marketing outlined in that book. My long, hard journey is now your shortcut, but only if you want to make more money while providing great value to others.

You see, long before the internet, direct response marketing was mostly confined to direct mail ("junk mail") and print advertisements. Today's spam is akin to yesteryear's junk mail. Today's ads on Facebook, LinkedIn, and other social media platforms aren't very different from these ads in the back of publications.

Different mediums to be sure, but the principles are the same.

In direct response marketing, you're either radically relevant or completely ignored. Honing my skills in this specialty drilled into me the absolute critical importance of marketing and sales strategies that are radically relevant.

"But I Don't Do Direct Response Marketing"

Is that what you were thinking the entire time I was telling this last story? Were you discounting the principles because you think your business is different?

Sorry, but you *are* in the direct response marketing business. Every business in every industry is in the response-creating business. The principles that work in direct response marketing are tried and true, and they can (and should) be applied to all areas of marketing, sales, and general influence.

Look . . . whenever you talk about your business, whether it's verbally at an event or face-to-face with a prospect, in writing on your website, through your LinkedIn profile, or an email, aren't you looking for a response directly related to what you said? Most of your communication should have what marketers label a *call to action* (CTA). If you are not including CTAs on most of your website pages and in most of your correspondence, you are probably missing many opportunities.

I've said it once and I'll probably say it a few more times in this book: You must be *radically relevant* to attract and maintain someone's interest. And you must be *critically compelling* to move them to action—whatever that action may be.

Never presume a prospect or client can read your mind and take the action you desire. If you want them to do something, ask them to do it!

RADICALLY RELEVANT ACTION STEPS

1. Head over to www.RadicalRelevanceToolkit.com to download the "8 Principles of Radical Relevance." Print it. Keep it visible.
2. Examine one of your recent marketing initiatives and evaluate it against the "8 Principles of Radical Relevance." Did you follow all seven? What kinds of results did the initiative produce? How could closer adherence to these principles improve your next marketing effort?

"Emails not being returned? Recommendations not being followed? Perhaps your messages are not relevant and compelling enough to create action."

—Bill Cates

RADICAL RULE OF RELEVANCE #2

Give your clients a seat at the table. Never develop services, product offers, or marketing messages without speaking to some of your clients. This is how you guarantee relevance.

CHAPTER 3

The Neuroscience of Relevance

I'm fascinated by science—learning the why behind the what. I'm particularly drawn to physics and most recently, neuroscience.

Yet, even though I find science captivating, I am in no way, shape, or form a scientist. So what's a guy who regularly skipped physics in high school doing writing about the science of relevance—particularly the neuroscience?

Neuroscience provides us with a window into the behavior of others and ourselves. You and I are in the influence business. We produce results for others by helping them make decisions that are in their best interest. Right? We are trying to grab the attention of others, so they'll listen to what we have to say. If the match is right, we are trying to compel them to work with us—knowing that if they do, we'll be of service to them. That's the way business works.

Applying some of the principles of neuroscience will transform your business.

The Brain and Relevance

The primary function of the brain is to keep the organism alive. As mentioned earlier, the brain is driven to help you move around and navigate your environment in a meaningful way. Our brains are dedicated to action. Brains do so by also looking for efficiencies of action. Why? To conserve energy—conserve calories. This is one reason the brain craves clarity. Confusion wastes energy and can be perceived as dangerous to the organism. The brain doesn't like that. Let me emphasize this again. The brain seeks clarity.

The brain also needs relevance to keep the organism alive. The amygdala (as part of the limbic/emotional center of the brain and as the chief relevance-detecting monitor in the brain) processes information from the environment rapidly to look for what is relevant to survival. A trusting face is relevant. So is an untrusting one. But the brain puts the danger triggers on top so that the frontal cortex can do something about the danger (whatever it may be).

The brain avoids danger, loves opportunity, seeks action, and craves clarity. There's your MBA in marketing right there. You're welcome.

There's more science to cover, but let's stop and apply this to business for a minute. Let's say that many of your prospects use airports. As they move through security and down corridors to the gate, they must navigate several hundred people coming at them, often getting in their way. They are also bombarded by marketing messages on the walls, hanging from the ceiling, and sometimes even on the floor. And all the while, their brains are scanning, scanning, scanning—faster than the speed of thought. Am I safe? Is this dangerous? Is this an opportunity? Ice cream would taste good right about now.

Once you know that your prospects' brains are constantly scanning for relevant dangers and relevant opportunities, to hit the bullseye in the brain, you must craft messaging that will make the brain feel safe, clear, and happy. That's marketing. That's sales. That's influence.

Scott Halford, author of *Activate Your Brain,* explains how this works.

He told me, "If you've ever met someone who you immediately knew you didn't like without a lot of words being said, that's (in part) the amygdala looking into its memory—its filing cabinet of every emotional experience you have experienced and matching it to the current experience. This person who does not resonate with you probably talked, acted, looked, and treated you like someone you've had a bad outcome with before. The obverse situation is true when you meet someone with whom you immediately resonate."

At the same time, he says, the amygdala is looking for traits it trusts in order to calm the threat response. The traits that we look for—trust, likability, engagement, confidence, credibility, and authenticity—resonate positively with us. Thus, memory plays an important role in relevance.

On the other hand, with the written word, we struggle to read emotion and safety accurately. That's why human interaction is so important in building trust. It's also why Halford advises us to avoid dealing with anything that is critical or substantial in a relationship through email or texting.

So if you're selling anything more than a simple product or service that doesn't require much thought, you have to stop hiding behind technology. No more thinking you can grow your business through email and web pages alone. It's much harder to build trust and gain influence that way. Even if you can't meet your prospects in person or face-to-face, you can use recorded videos and online chats to make a human connection.

Where Does Trust Come In?

For someone to do business with you, they must trust you. But first, your message must resonate with them, or they will simply ignore you. They must perceive what you are saying as relevant to them at that moment in time. If you're not relevant, you'll be ignored. (And no one likes to be ignored.)

Once you've grabbed someone's attention and continue to remain relevant, you can start working on building trust. Halford says it this way, "Trust is safety. Trust is knowing what to expect from a situation or person.

Trust is extraordinarily positive. It is also fleeting. If I trust you and you are inconsistent, even one time, you can break the safety that leads to trust."

Emotion Moves the World

Author Jimmy Breslin, who was quite adept at striking an emotional chord with words, once said, "It all comes down to emotion. Emotion moves the world."

Neuroscience backs this up. The renowned neuroscientist Antonio Damasio used technology known as magnetic resonance tomography (MRT) to study subjects with damage in the part of the brain that experienced emotion. What he discovered is important to our examination of relevance and persuasion. Subjects who couldn't experience emotion couldn't make a decision. No emotion equals no decision (or, at best, a bad decision).

So Breslin was right. Emotion rules the world. It's emotion that creates the action in a relationship. This is not to say that the prefrontal cortex and the processing of information aren't important. Of course, it is. But emotion is at the heart of every decision.

If you want your prospects and clients to follow your suggestions and recommendations, you must strike an emotional response in them. No emotion, no action.

In Part 4, I will show you how to create that emotional connection that moves people to action.

Offer Clarity or Certainty

According to Jeff Hawkins, an inventor and founder of the Redwood Center for Theoretical Neuroscience, "Your brain receives patterns from the outside world, stores them as memories, and makes predictions by combining what it has seen before and what is happening now . . . Prediction . . . is the primary function of the neo-cortex, and the foundation of intelligence." When the craving for certainty is met, he says, there is a sensation of reward.

It's no wonder, then, that we often find it challenging to get our prospects and clients to follow our recommendations. Their brains hate uncertainty. Said another way, "The devil they know is better than the devil they don't know."

When a situation is unclear or uncertain, an alert goes off in the brain's amygdala to pay more attention. That uncertainty leads to discomfort, something we tend to avoid.

This tells me that helping your prospects and clients become clear or certain about their current and/or future situation can be a very relevant and compelling aspect of how you shape the messaging around your value.

Memory's Role in This

Impossible to Ignore by Carmen Simon reveals that communication is only effective if the message sticks in the minds of the listeners long enough to influence their choice at the decision point. This supports my contention that you can't just capture the attention of prospects or clients and then forget about it. You must *remain relevant* throughout your interactions with them.

Memory guides their actions in three ways:

1. To repeat actions that were rewarding for them in the past.
2. To modify past actions in light of new information.
3. To instinctively pursue courses of action that ensure their biological fitness (i.e., survival).

In her book, Simon shares what you probably already know: "Research indicates that about 60 to 80 percent of memory problems involve forgetting to perform a future intention. You may remember to execute the intention later but fail to act on it because the motivation is no longer there. In the same vein, your audience may agree that your proposal is helpful but fail to respond appropriately because the reward is not sufficient."

Therefore, you want your messaging to provide your prospects and clients with a glimpse of future value—what their future will look and feel like once their problem has been solved or their goal attained. Anticipate their future and tailor your message around their future intention, so they will remember and act on it later.

This is something I've been doing with my messaging for quite some time. In some situations, I help my audience anticipate future obstacles they may encounter, whether they're logistical, emotional, or social. Then I give them tools to move those obstacles aside.

According to Simon, the brain seeks to maximize reward and to minimize effort and risk. How does this play out in your messaging? You have to position the final outcome—the problem solved or goal attained—in a way that won't require a huge amount of effort. If that just isn't practical or honest, you must provide them with the promise of other rewards that can come more quickly.

Your prospects will execute on your suggestions based on the effort they have to make, risk they must bear, and how long they'll have to wait until they get rewards. As you'll see in Chapter 20, your prospects will usually be more motivated to spend time and dollars on a critical goal than they will when the goal is aspirational.

For example, a financial advisor may tout the reward of enjoying a comfortable retirement without fear of running out of money. But if the prospect is younger, that reward is so far into their future, the motivation to save appropriately may wane. The advisor can address this by creating interim milestones for the client to achieve and by finding simple ways to reward those shorter-term goals.

Start with Familiar Messaging

For the past 25 years, I've been instinctively coaching clients to position their messaging to address concepts that are already present in their prospects' brains. I've explained that if you introduce an unfamiliar concept too quickly, you run the risk of lacking relevance, because you're asking them to work too hard.

I'm now proud to proclaim that brain science supports what I've been saying all along. (Don't you love it when you're right about something?) It goes something like this: The brains of your targets prefer familiar concepts because it takes less processing energy to grasp those concepts. Carmen Simon, author of *Impossible to Ignore*, points out that, "Familiar things allow the brain to let its guard down and derive pleasure from accurate predictions. Find out what your listeners (prospects and clients) are familiar with and feed them that content first to get more of their attention."

Then, you can bring in a more novel, counterintuitive, or surprising concept to peak their attention.

Then, Break the Pattern

Interrupting the familiar can be accomplished in a number of ways. Use a contrarian or controversial headline or a made-up word. When doing the latter, be careful. If you haven't established some context first (familiarity), the new word may require too much brain-processing power. That's when you risk losing your audience. Chapter 15 will cover this concept of interrupting the familiar in more detail.

RADICALLY RELEVANT ACTION STEPS

1. Assess if you might be relying too much on technology (email, website, social media, etc.) to make a solid connection with prospects. See how you can insert the human connection into your marketing plan.
2. When you write marketing messages, do your best to strike an emotional response with prospects and clients.
3. Make sure all (or most) of your messaging begins with something that is familiar to the recipient before introducing a new concept.

"It all comes down to emotion. Emotion moves the world."

—Jimmy Breslin, American Journalist and Author

PART 2

Strategic Relevance

Now that we've established a case for radical relevance, let's continue by covering some of the strategic decisions you need to make before you can get tactical with your messaging.

I believe it's a mistake to think of your value proposition as merely a short statement about your business that you can use to answer the question, "What do you do?"

We'll start with an important exercise that you, and everyone in your firm, can perform to discover your full value. Then, we'll work on narrowing your focus until you can identify and hit the bullseye for your business, i.e., your Right-Fit Client.

RADICAL RULE OF RELEVANCE #3

Value is in the eye of the beholder. It's your job to determine, develop, and communicate your value in a way that will resonate with the prospects who are a perfect fit for your business.

CHAPTER 4

Discover Your Complete Value Proposition

Value proposition . . . unique value proposition . . . unique selling proposition . . . brand positioning statement . . . elevator pitch . . .

You've heard these terms before. Are they simply different names for the same thing? The short answer is "No!"

While some people will tell you that a value proposition is a short statement or promise of your value, I strongly disagree.

Your value proposition is the total of *all* the value you bring to prospects, clients, strategic partnerships, and—yes—even employees. Your value proposition is the basis of your relevance.

Your value proposition is the most fundamental aspect of your business. With no clear and coherent value proposition, you have no business. Your *elevator pitch*, your *unique selling proposition*, *brand positioning statement*, or your *statement of differentiation* are simply different ways of communicating select aspects of your value proposition to others.

Is Your Brand the Same as Your Value Proposition?

During speeches and workshops, I am often asked about the relationship between brand and value proposition.

Rather than guess, I consulted with branding expert Bruce Turkel, author of *Building Brand Value* and *All About Them*. He said there's no specific, agreed-upon definition to either term—brand or value proposition.

"As I see it, your value proposition and your brand should be the same thing. That is, you're known not only for who you are and what you do but for what you mean to your customer/client/consumer/community," he told me, citing a few brand examples with their value propositions:

- Volvo = safety (and now, safety with luxury)
- Starbucks = getting together
- Jeep = rugged
- Tumi = sophisticated travel

What we think of when we see these brands isn't their product function—it's their attributes that then get transferred, more or less, to their users.

Some mistakenly think that a brand is a logo or a tagline. Turkel offers an accurate definition: "A brand is our reputation, the promise we make to our clients/customers, the feeling our clients/customers get when they consume our products or services, etc. All of these interactions should both promise and deliver our value proposition—that's why brand and value proposition should be synonymous."

This means you can't have one without the other—and they must be consistent. Your brand should reflect your full value proposition; how you communicate that value proposition should be congruent and consistent with your brand.

3-Phase Approach to Building Your Complete Value Proposition

When is the last time you and your team stopped to take inventory of the comprehensive value you bring to prospects, clients, and strategic partnerships?

Before developing your clever elevator pitch, business card slogan, or website positioning statement, I highly recommend getting clear on your complete value proposition. Involving everyone in your organization in this endeavor will help rally everybody around your value. It will have a positive impact on your overall culture while it equips people with better ways to communicate the organization's value to virtually anyone they meet.

Here are three steps you and everyone in your organization can take to develop your complete value proposition.

1. **Assess your full value.**

   Not by yourself, but with as many team members as possible, go through all the processes you bring to client relationships—from first contact through courtship and onboarding. Include how you serve and bring value over the lifetime of the relationship. Make note of all the points of value that you bring: questions you ask, what you teach, services you render, opportunities you present, and—especially—problems that you solve.

   This is the sort of attention to detail that will give you and everyone in your organization a clear view of the incredible value you deliver in all relationship phases with prospects and clients. But don't stop there.

2. **Get your clients involved.**

   Show the work that you did in step one to a few key clients. Get their feedback and impressions. You'll be amazed at how much you will learn and the ideas they will offer about communicating your value—insights that would never occur to you.

For example, as I was doing this exercise with my own business, a client said, "Bill Cates makes asking for referrals as natural as breathing." Wow! Not bad, eh? I never would have thought about messaging my value in that way.

3. **Blend your work.**
   Combine and consolidate the work you've done in the first two steps to create a comprehensive, but concise, expression of your value proposition. This can be a numbered or bulleted list of all the steps in your relationships and the value those steps bring.

   Share this document with all current and new team members as you bring them into your organization. Note, though, that it's unlikely you will share this entire document with any prospects or clients. This is for internal use.

With this important work in place, you are now in a good position to identify the various ways you want to communicate your value.

Where Do You Communicate Your Value?

You communicate your value *everywhere*: your website, social media, printed materials, voice mail and email messages, and in-person when networking or attending community events, client functions, and even social gatherings. Just about everything you speak or write will in some way reflect and communicate your value proposition. Let's look at some of the components that go into messaging or communicating your value proposition.

First and foremost: Why do you communicate your value proposition? To answer this question, I have a bit of a pop quiz for you. Ready?

Is the purpose of communicating your value proposition to:

A. Help people understand what you do?
B. Attract the right people?
C. Repel the wrong people away from you?
D. Create action—to get them to respond to your communication?
E. Help people realize that you are the right fit for their situation so they'll continue to follow your recommendations and requests?

What did you choose? A, B, C, D, or E? Or maybe you wanted to choose all of them?

If you thought "all of the above," you'd be right.

How you communicate your value must be as *relevant* as possible, so that you will gain and retain interest. How you communicate your value must be *compelling* to move people to action.

And how you communicate your value proposition must create a sense of mutual fit. At the end of the day, after all is said and done, what your prospect really wants to know is, "Are you the right fit for me?" They want to feel confident that the decision to work with you is the right one. How you communicate your value must be designed to cause *just the right prospects* to make that decision to become your clients.

The Whole is Greater Than the Sum of Its Parts

It was in my early childhood, about 384 BC, when Aristotle told me, "Bill, remember this: The whole is greater than the sum of its parts." I know, I'm dating myself with reference to Aristotle's mentorship, and I'm not usually one to name drop. Nevertheless, this famous quote is perfect for this chapter.

I've identified seven primary components that form a complete value proposition from which you can create powerful messaging—messaging that will be *radically relevan*t to attract and sustain interest, and *critically compelling* to move people to action (like respond to your email or become your client). When you put them together, you'll see what Aristotle meant in our conversation.

Your 7 Steps to a Complete Value Proposition

We'll begin with a graphic representation of these steps followed by a brief overview of each component. Some of these steps are covered in greater detail in this book; the others can be found at www.RadicalRelevanceToolkit.com.

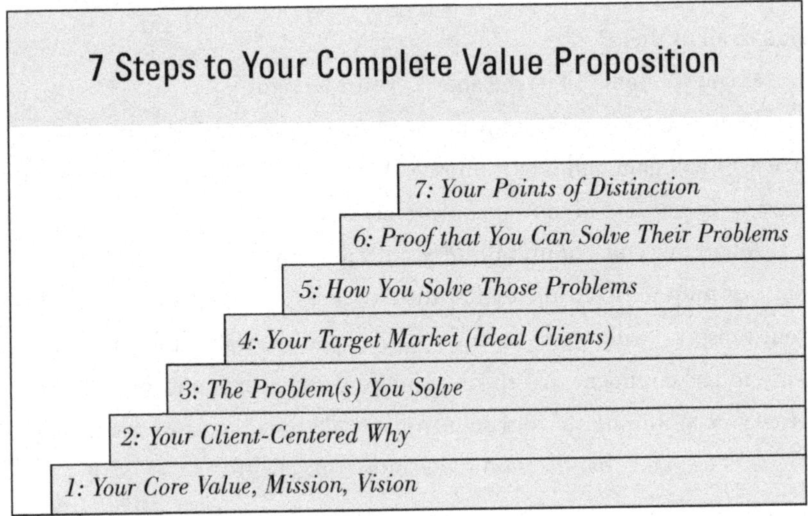

Figure 3

Step 1: Your Core Values, Mission, Vision

If your value proposition is the foundation of your business success, then your core values, mission, and vision make up the first building blocks of that foundation. A value proposition that incorporates these three elements will likely be more effective than one that doesn't. These fundamentals are not only the cornerstones of your value proposition, they're the cornerstones of your entire business culture. One could argue that these two concepts—your organization's culture and value proposition—are inseparable. One informs and impacts the other for both your internal culture and how your brand is perceived by your prospects and clients.

For more on this important component of your complete value proposition, go to www.RadicalRelevanceToolkit.com for the report titled, *Core Values, Vision, and Mission.*

"WE LET OUR VISION GUIDE US IN WHAT WE WOULD DO AND DON'T DO."

The Provident Bank, located in Amesbury, Mass., is an innovative commercial bank. I had the pleasure of working with its commercial banking consultants to help them generate more clients through referrals and introductions and to refine their value proposition.

Bank President Chuck Withee continually works to make his institution stand out from competitors. Because its sole focus is on commercial banking, Provident delivers the services and products of larger organizations, but with the personalized touch of a local banker.

When we talked about relevance for this book, Chuck said, "Several years ago, we realized that as a community bank, if we tried to be all things to all people, we couldn't have an authentic and unique value proposition. Being all things to all people would be a race to the bottom."

Then, he made an astute and important observation about unique selling propositions (USPs). "Your USPs cannot be aspirational," he said, "because you don't have supporting evidence. And they can't be platitudes that everyone else uses, or they're not unique. So we made the game-changing decision that not everybody is our ideal client."

(Continued)

Chuck and his team decided to focus on just the business side of banking. The board of directors was nervous initially, but Chuck and his team were confident they were making the right decision.

As part of the information-gathering process for this change, Chuck's team interviewed clients, as well as all of the employees. He knew he had to empower everyone at every level to execute on the ideas that fit the vision.

"When you are truly unique in your expertise, the platitudes go out the window. Your differentiation is real and authentic," he said.

When we talked about what it means to be compelling, Chuck told me, "The key is knowing your prospects' and clients' pain points. To do this, you must ask good, penetrating questions with a listening heart. If there is real pain, and you show that you can fix it, you stand a chance of winning their business. But their pain must be big enough for them to want to move away from it—to make a change in their status quo. If their pain is tolerable, they'll think, 'That's okay. I'll continue to suffer.' "

Chuck also offered an excellent tactic to use when a prospect acknowledges the pain but doesn't seem to want to act. His consultants respond with, "You say you would like the problem to go away, but you seem unwilling to take any action. Can you see my dilemma?" Brilliant!

You must be willing to shine a bright light on how you can legitimately help clients face their challenges and have the courage to initiate a candid conversation.

Step 2: Your Client-Focused Why

There are many ways to think about your "why." It could be why you wake up in the morning; the overarching purpose for your being. (Wow—that's heavy!)

It could be why you do the work you do in a purely self-serving way. For example, many financial advisors get into the business because they enjoy dealing with financial matters, they want a more flexible schedule, and they can usually make darn good money. And I have no problem with that "why."

By a *client-focused why*, though, I'm referring to why you believe in your value. I'm talking about *why you believe in the work you do*—why it's important to both you and your clients. Sometimes your company mission can be inspired by your client-centered why or vice versa. Either way, they are close cousins.

For more on this important component of your complete value proposition, go to www.RadicalRelevanceToolkit.com for *Your Client-Focused Why*.

Step 3: The Problems You Solve/Opportunities You Capture

Which comes first—the problems you solve (and your product/service that does the work) or your target market? Well, you tell me. Would you rather have a product/service in search of a market, or a clearly defined market to which you bring highly relevant products, processes, and services? With that said, maybe you already have a product and/or service for which you're trying to grow revenue and profits.

Some successful businesses study their target market carefully, asking questions about challenges and problems without yet having the solutions. Then, they create products or services that either address an unmet need or offer a solution that's better than anything available.

Regardless of how you start this process, you want to be very clear about the problems you solve and opportunities you present to your target market.

I'll go into much more detail on solving problems later in the book.

Step 4: Your Target Market

Having a target market is the most basic of marketing principles. It's hard to hit the bullseye and score big points (or big dollars) without a clear target. Generally speaking, the narrower your target, the better. Your marketing efforts will be more effective because you'll be bullseye-relevant and you'll be much better at solving client problems and helping them maximize opportunities.

I'll probably say this a few times in this book: "If you try to appeal to everyone, you run the risk of appealing to no one."

And never forget that a market is made up of people. On a strategic level, we can think in terms of solving one or more problems for a market, industry, or business. But if we don't drill down to the personas (the people) that make up the market, we'll come up short in communicating our value with relevance.

Having the right target market and knowing your persona (Right-Fit Client) are such fundamental components of winning more ideal clients that I devote significant discussion to these concepts later in the book.

Step 5: How You Solve Those Problems

What services and/or products do you offer that deliver value—that solve your clients' problems or maximize their opportunities? How do you implement your value?

Do you start with an assessment, share the results, recommend next steps? Do you charge for that assessment? Do you create a robust plan and charge for it? Do you have a client onboarding process? Do you have a client service promise where you continue to provide value over time?

How you solve problems and maximize opportunities is at the core of your value proposition. The *how* is what does the work. The challenge I see for many is that they are so enamored with their product/service that they spend an inordinate amount of time describing its features. They don't spend nearly enough time getting to know the prospect first—establishing enough context to make their messaging more relevant (to attract interest). Likewise, they don't spend enough time discussing benefits their product/service delivers—benefits that can help compel that prospect to action.

Perhaps you've heard this trite, but true, expression, "Customers don't buy the drill; they buy the hole they want to make." Same is true for you and me. Be careful about being so enamored with your offering that you neglect to create relevance and translate features into clear benefits. I will cover that piece in more detail in the next chapter.

Step 6: Proof That You Can Solve Their Problems

When you sell a product or service that is complicated or intangible, you're selling trust. Therefore, you need a body of evidence that provides proof that you can do what you say you can. One of the best sources of this is an introduction from someone your prospect already trusts. Sometimes that's enough; sometimes you need more to move them to act. I go into more detail on building your body of evidence later in the book.

Step 7: Your Points of Distinction

What makes you different? What separates your value proposition from your competitor's? How important is it for you to have an answer to this question? Do your prospects and clients care about what makes you different? I'll dig into this important topic in the next chapter.

Your Right-Fit Clients

When someone is considering doing business with you, the decision usually boils down to this key question: "Is this the right fit for me?" This decision process should go both ways—you need to determine if they are the right fit for you, too. For most businesses, in fact, this should be a mutual consideration.

See if you can relate to this. You go into a store that sells large flat-screen televisions. You see more than 20 of them mounted on the wall. You narrow it down to three or four. Then, you're stuck. You read all the descriptions, and they're either all pretty much the same or use terms you don't fully understand. If you're lucky enough to find a knowledgeable department employee, that person can usually tilt the scale by asking you a few questions you might not have considered.

For just about every buying decision I can think of, it comes down to the prospects saying to themselves, "This feels right. This is the best fit more me; this meets my needs or goals." A radically relevant value proposition will help you and your prospects get to a decision on fit faster.

RADICALLY RELEVANT ACTION STEPS

1. Schedule time to work with others in your firm on the "3-Phase Approach to Building Your Complete Value Proposition." I guarantee that this will be time well-invested. When you have it figured out, work to get everyone in your organization on the same page with your full value.
2. Examine your website, LinkedIn profile, and any tool you use to communicate your value. Are you merely describing what you do, or are you trying to attract the right people, repel the wrong people, and move them to take specific action?
3. Review the "7 Steps to Your Complete Value Proposition." What work do you and others in your organization need to do to strengthen each of these areas?

"Looking different in the marketplace isn't about what you or your company does. It's about what your clients receive *from what you do."*

—Ardath Albee, in her book Digital Relevance

CHAPTER 5

What Makes You Different?

Many businesses struggle to understand and articulate what makes them different. But let's be clear about one thing: **Your prospects don't care about what makes you different unless they see exactly how that difference benefits them.**

Superficial differences might attract attention, but if there isn't an immediately recognizable tangible value associated with that difference, your differentiation will not accomplish your goal of acquiring more clients.

If you take the time to develop a complete value proposition as described in the previous chapter, "What makes you different?" should be an easy question to answer. Doing the recommended exercises will help unearth or clarify those differences. For example, if you focus exclusively on a narrow target market (covered in detail in Chapter 6), that can easily be turned into a point of distinction with a clear set of benefits for prospects and clients.

Your processes—how you do what you do—might be your main point of distinction. Also, your client-focused why might be what you can use to set yourself apart.

Remember: Trying to discover and communicate what makes you different is merely an academic exercise with little to no value until you turn that difference into a clear and important benefit for prospects and clients.

Relevant Differentiation

How many times has someone told you about their product or service without taking time to find out if what they offered was even relevant to you?

At the very least, you should attempt to learn a few things about your prospect's world, then tailor how you communicate your value based on that information. This includes determining which differentiators to use in your communication.

Your Sources of Differentiation

If a high-level prospect or potential center of influence asks what makes you different, do you have an immediate, succinct, and confident answer? Do you struggle, or are you confident?

Here are five broad categories to help you discover all of your points of distinction in a manner that provides real value:

1. **Expertise or Specialization**
   People like to work with experts and specialists. Expertise can come from formal education, certifications, and years of experience. Don't be timid about emphasizing your expertise and how you specialize.

2. **Target Market**
   When you focus on a target market, your value is often perceived immediately because of the questions you ask and the

concepts you choose to discuss. When you focus on a specific market, you can demonstrate immediate empathy for their challenges and opportunities, often bringing solutions that a generalist just can't offer.

3. **Process for Discovering and Revealing Problems and Opportunities**
   Employing a comprehensive approach to discussing your prospects' and clients' problems can be a great source of value. For example, your discovery process might reveal problems and opportunities that were previously hidden to the prospect. Your discovery process can bring value quickly in a new relationship by getting prospects to think in ways they haven't before.

4. **Process for Customizing and Delivering Solutions**
   Once you conduct a comprehensive discovery process and truly know the context in which you find prospects and clients, you are in position to bring truly customized remedies to their problems and help maximize their opportunities.

5. **Process for Adding Continual Value to Clients**
   One of your points of differentiation may stem from how you continually bring value to your clients. While some of these points might be included in your core offering, others may be value-added items that surprise and delight clients, such as client-appreciation events. Communicating your client service promise to prospects can often be the tipping point that turns that person into a client.

"This is Our Client Service Promise"

Jennifer Reese is a financial advisor in Ohio who has done a great job of defining and communicating her client service promise. Jennifer told me a story about how sharing her client service promise with a prospect won her a new client.

Jennifer said to the prospect, "I'd like to tell you a little bit about our client service promise. In addition to our quarterly review meetings, we host a number of educational opportunities for our clients, as well as regular, fun client-appreciation events. For example . . ."

As Jennifer was beginning to go into more detail about her client service promise, the prospect interrupted her and said, "Wait a second. You mean to tell me that this is how you've been staying in touch with my friend Rick all the years he's been with you?

"It sure is," Jennifer replied. "This is our client service promise."

To which the prospect said, "I think the only time I hear from my advisor is when I call him!"

Two weeks later, this prospect became a client and brought in $2.5 million for Jennifer to manage.

Your points of differentiation are often simple—and right in front of you. When you're clear on them, you'll communicate them with the kind of confidence that sparks interest and trust.

Turning Differentiation into Benefits

Here are two common mistakes I see people make when it comes to communicating their points of distinction:

Big Mistake #1: Platitudes

If your competitors are saying it, or just about anyone in your type of business can say it, it's a platitude and not a differentiator.

When I present speeches and workshops, I ask audience members,

"Do you ever use 'great client service' as a way to standout?" The non-scientific result is that 75 percent of these folks raise their hands.

If most businesses attempt to use great service to differentiate, guess what? They're not standing out. At least not until they put a little more meat on that statement's bones. (After all, every client expects great service.)

If most people can claim it, it's a platitude. Phrases like "great service," "responsive service," "we care about our customers," and the like are not differentiators unless you provide specific examples that demonstrate how your service would exceed anyone's expectations.

Don't get me wrong—I'm not saying you shouldn't tell prospects that you provide great service or personalized attention. Just make sure you make it more than a platitude by translating that feature into a clear benefit. Providing a specific example can help with that.

Big Mistake #2: Benefits Aren't Clear or Obvious

Over the years, I've done a fair amount of work in the financial services industry. When one of my banking clients gave me a list of the institution's unique selling propositions (USPs), I noticed immediately that with few exceptions, they weren't translated into clear benefits.

I advised the bank to turn these USPs into benefits that will be meaningful to potential clients because prospects won't take the time to figure this out for themselves. On the following page are a few of the bank's USPs and the team's work to translate them into benefits.

In reality, most features can be tied to these benefits: making or saving money, saving time, reducing stress, providing clarity, and gaining confidence.

USP (Bank Feature)	Benefit	Comment
7-Point Process We review a seven-point checklist with our clients each year that includes a 360-degree view of how we are doing for them.	The checklist and 360-degree review give us a real-time report card from our clients, which always leads to even better service for them. Better service = happier client.	Proprietary processes and checklists are a great way to distinguish yourself from competitors. If you name and trademark your process, then only you can own it and use.
Stability We have a unique ownership structure that prevents us from being acquired by another bank.	This means continuity, reliability, and stability for our clients. Stability = trust.	This is a particularly important benefit to communicate when an industry is in flux.
Award-Winning Bank Top SBA 7a lender for three consecutive years; named 504 lender of the year for several years.	When it comes to taking care of the unique needs of small and medium size businesses, we have the tools and creativity to get it done. Done right = confidence.	Winning awards means you're doing something right. But never assume your prospects or clients know how your awards directly benefit them.
Simplicity We simplify complex transactions.	The bank has a collaborative team of commercial experts to provide customized financial solutions that make clients' lives easier. Makes life easier = less stress.	I'm a big fan of the words *simplicity* and *clarity*. If your world is filled with complicated information or processes, the promise of clarity and simplicity is an attractive benefit.
Continuity Our lenders have worked with their customers 12 times longer than the industry average.	Our clients don't have to waste their time educating new bankers about their situation. Less wasted time = happier clients.	Saving time or preventing wasted time is a compelling benefit.

STANDING OUT IN A COMMODITY INDUSTRY

"What differentiates our business is our commitment to the long-term relationship in an industry where that is usually ignored," said Craig Strent, CEO of Apex Home Loans (www.ApexHomelLoans.com) in Rockville, Md., over breakfast as I was interviewing him for this book.

"I tell clients, 'If you work with me, you'll never worry about your mortgage again. We'll send quarterly reports letting you know if it's time to refinance. We manage your mortgage for you," he said.

Craig has used this approach to take his business to levels most mortgage companies only dream about.

His company's trigger point came around December 2007, when the housing market collapsed and sent many homes into foreclosure. It also sent plenty of real estate agents and mortgage originators looking for new employment.

The collapse took most industry professionals by surprise.

"Sometimes change in an industry can come so fast that you'll wake up one day and wonder what planet you're on. We must always be ready to justify, defend, or reframe our value to our prospects and customers, or we'll die a fast death in the marketplace," Craig said.

He and his partners not only weathered the economic storm that hit them hard, they slowly but surely began to grow. His company has continued to grow because they built a business designed to deliver a better experience.

This is reflected in the firm's mission: "We deliver a superior home financing experience through a better mortgage process and lifelong mortgage management."

The company even has a chief experience officer, Steve Dorfman. Now I ask you, how many small to mid-sized companies have a chief experience officer? Steve knows that a company's ability to provide a great customer experience starts with the employee work experience.

(Continued)

He once told me, "The external experience that we are able to provide our customers is a reflection of our own internal culture."

"Without question, this shift and commitment to delivering a better experience is the single most important thing we've done to create a thriving business," Craig said. "Our prospects tell us they can feel the difference from the very beginning and our customers can't believe that we are really staying in touch with them to keep the experience and value coming."

Craig knows that businesses trapped in "commodity thinking" pay attention to client satisfaction. Businesses that separate themselves focus on client experience.

A Tagline is Not a Value Positioning Statement

In his article, "Useful Value Proposition Examples and How to Create One," (http://bit.ly/2Kwbqdi) Peep Laja makes the point that the tagline that accompanies your logo, or a slogan in the banner of your website, is not your value positioning statement.

Since your tagline or slogan should be totally congruent with your value positioning statement and overall value proposition, this very short statement will often be a shorter version of your value positioning statement.

As you'll see in the first two examples below, taglines or slogans can often hold very little meaning without further elaboration.

Bitly (https://bitly.com) is a web application that allows you to shorten a long URL. At this writing, the company's slogan is "Links that mean business." This statement on its own gives you no insight into the product. Scroll just a little bit, though, and you'll see: "Get the edge you need with links you can trust. Bitly helps you maximize the impact of every digital initiative with industry-leading features and tools." That's a benefit.

Slack (https://slack.com) is a web application that facilitates communication between teams or groups. At this writing, its website declares, "Whatever work you do, you can do it in Slack." That's doubtful if, say, you repair motorcycles, right? But right below that slogan is: "Slack gives your team the power and alignment you need to do your best work." That helps it get closer to a benefit.

Convince & Convert (https://convinceandconvert.com) is content marketing expert Jay Baer's website. His banner tagline reads: "We Help You Connect With Your Customers." Now that's a tagline that conveys some insight and benefit. The text under the headline includes, "We help interesting companies create effective strategies for customer acquisition and retention." Bingo! A great one-two punch from a meaningful tagline followed by a clear benefit.

In Chapter 12, I will show you how to incorporate one or more of your meaningful differences into how you reach out to new prospects.

RADICALLY RELEVANT ACTION STEPS

1. With your staff or team members, create a list of all the points of differentiation you would like to communicate to prospects, clients, and strategic alliances. Remember to stay away from platitudes such as "great client service" unless you can quickly back that up with one or more specific examples.
2. Take that list and articulate tangible benefits your prospects and/or clients will derive from each point of distinction.
3. Talk to several clients with whom you can discuss the results of this exercise to get their input on how they perceive your differences and what those differences mean to them.

RADICAL RULE OF RELEVANCE #4

Meet your prospects where they are. Before talking about the journey of transformation you will create for your clients, find out where they are in that journey. Everyone who comes to you will be at a different place—their place.

CHAPTER 6

Create the Right Target

Picture an archery target bulging with straw stuffing. It features concentric rings of black, blue, and red that lead your eye to the bright yellow bullseye.

Are you ready for the big metaphor? The archery target represents your target market. If you have more than one target market, simply visualize more than one target. Each target demands that your messaging be geared specifically for it—it can't be generic. Otherwise, your messaging will be watered down—possibly to the point of being totally ineffective.

This chapter presents concepts about the power of selecting and serving a clearly defined target market—also called a niche or vertical market. The more targeted your market, the more relevant your messaging will naturally become. If you already have one or more target markets, let's fine-tune your awareness, strategies, and tactics. If you don't yet have a clear target market, these ideas will be critical to your expanded success.

Once I address the target market concept as a whole, I'll turn your attention to hitting the bullseye. It represents your ideal or Right-Fit Client—the clients you were meant to serve and who were meant to be served by you.

Riches in the Niches

Niche marketing . . . target marketing . . . vertical marketing . . .

These are not new concepts to you, but . . . are you truly leveraging the considerable power of target marketing to find more clients to serve, more revenue to generate, and more dollars in your bank account?

You may be wondering, "If target marketing is so effective, why don't more professionals and businesses fully engage in this powerful strategy?" In two words: mistaken assumption.

The mistaken assumption that inhibits others from getting rich with a niche is this: "If I only focus on this target market to the exclusion of others, I'll give up sizable opportunities." The reality is that, yes, you may miss other opportunities, but you'll be so successful in your target market that you'll hardly notice—and you won't care. Plus, when you decide to focus on a narrow market, you don't have to fire current clients or even turn down other business. Over time, however, you might find yourself only accepting Right-Fit Clients.

8 Massive Benefits of Defining or Narrowing Your Target Market

Because pursuing a smaller audience is counterintuitive, people are often surprised by the many benefits offered by this strategy. Here are eight of them.

1. **Target marketing makes it easier to identify your prospects.** In our increasingly digital world, you can find lists that include contact information for people in just about any prospect category you want. And as you probably know, LinkedIn is one of the best search engines for discovering relevant prospects. When you use it to identify connections between prospects and current clients who might be willing to introduce you, you'll see how working in a vertical market is much more effective.

2. **Target marketing allows you to bring more real value.**
   While your *perceived* value will be higher right from the start, so too will be your *real* value.

   For example, I recently presented to an audience of professionals who specialize in agricultural banking and insurance. The most successful of these folks don't see themselves as bankers or agents. They're "farm policy consultants" and "agricultural business consultants." This is precisely what separates them from the competition and brings tangible value to prospects and clients. Not surprisingly, their production and referral numbers are the highest in the industry.

3. **Target marketing helps you deliver a more relevant marketing message.**
   Your prospects' and clients' brains are constantly taking in information and instantly deciding, "Is this relevant to me?" They not only *need* your message to be relevant in order to grab their attention, they *expect* it to be.

   The narrower your focus, the more exacting your messaging becomes—on your website, LinkedIn profile, emails to prospects, and in conversations. The more exacting your message, the better able you are to attract the right people while repelling the wrong ones. Yes—you want to be compelling and repelling at the same time.

   More specific messaging adds to your credibility, too. Both the questions you ask and what you communicate, "This person knows my world." For example, Kyle Gregory is an extremely successful financial advisor who focuses on physicians and dentists in Charlotte, N.C. He reads their industry publications and has learned a few of the insurance medical codes. He can literally talk their language. "Hey, Doctor Smith. I'm having a real 308.9 today!" (Unspecified acute reaction to stress.)

4. **Target marketing helps you become super referable faster.**
When you focus on a specific niche market, you know that world better, so you're able to bring better solutions to their problems. Heck, you will know problems they have that they don't even know they have. This isn't just perceived value. This is *real* value. You will ask better questions and be more precise in your advice and solutions.

5. **Referrals and introductions will become easy and natural for you.**
Your clients know people just like themselves. And because you are more referable, referrals and introductions will be easier to generate. As clients see more and more people in their industry working with you, they will instinctively want to introduce you to more of them. Introducing you to others also validates their decision to work with you.

6. **You'll be able to leverage others targeting the same market.**
Every business or industry has what Ivan Misner, founder of Business Network International—better known as BNI—calls "contact spheres." They're also known as centers of influence, those who have the ability to introduce you to ideal clients but may have not experienced your value firsthand. They work with many of your clients and prospects and can send people your way. For example, financial planners, advisors, and insurance agents covet introductions from CPAs and attorneys—and vice versa.

    Luke Wiley is an extremely successful Cincinnati-based financial advisor who built most of his business targeting one large employer in his hometown. Luke has created quite a reputation for himself as the go-to advisor for the company's executives and upper-level managers. They tell him when new execs are hired and when others start thinking about retirement. Others in companion industries also focus on this particular company, so thanks to relationships Luke has formed with them, the employees they refer to Luke are always interested and qualified.

7. **You'll create a reputation for yourself.**

It's difficult to create a reputation for yourself when you have a shotgun approach to marketing. Creating visibility for yourself and/or your company is much easier when you go after a well-defined target market.

Professional organizations often have several formal and informal ways of gathering information and communicating with each other. If you provide value first, you'll be invited to participate in their activities that might include monthly meetings or networking events. For a much more in-depth discussion on how to create a reputation within a target market, head over to www.RadicalRelevanceToolkit.com.

8. **Your business will be more profitable.**

When you combine the power of creating a reputation for yourself with bringing more real value to prospects and clients, you can often charge more for some of your services. For example, a financial advisor can charge a premium for the planning process.

A friend of mine runs an extremely successful residential painting company. His target market is wealthy neighborhoods in a specific Maryland county. He once told me that when he first meets with homeowners to gather information for an estimate, they often say, "I hear you're really expensive, but worth every penny. Let me show you where I'd like you to start." In these situations, price is not an issue.

Because word of mouth, referrals, and introductions are easier to obtain and your messaging is stronger, your revenue will increase even though you're not spending more on marketing. It's a beautiful thing!

5 Profitable Target Market Attributes

You want to choose your target market carefully. Here are five attributes of a viable target market:

1. **The big problems are already identified.**
   The perfect target market is comprised of individuals and/or businesses who know they have a problem and understand its impact on their business, will admit to it, and really want to fix it. Yes, you can also have success uncovering and solving problems that prospects aren't yet aware of, but that takes more time. (More on this in Chapter 7.)

2. **They can afford you.**
   Regardless of the nature of your business, if a high percentage of the prospects in a niche don't have the financial capacity to take full advantage of your value, then it's probably the wrong niche for you.

3. **They have several ways of communicating formally and informally.**
   This means that people in the target market have networking and professional development opportunities that include meetings, events, publications, online forums, and other ways they gather physically and/or digitally. It might be through association or organization memberships, or through less formal structures. This allows you to build a visible reputation by actively participating alongside them.

4. **It's big enough.**
   Generally speaking, the narrower the niche, the better, as long as it's large enough for you to build and maintain your successful business. There may be subcategories or closely aligned markets that will make your market large enough.

5. **You enjoy working with your target market.**
   There's no point in investing time and effort to establish your reputation in a market you don't enjoy. In fact, if it's not a positive experience for you, you're less likely to become very successful anyway. There will always be a nagging voice saying, "Why did I pick this niche? I don't even like these people."

I strongly urge you to pick a target market that hits on all five of these criteria, if possible.

One Target at a Time

Once you've identified target markets, you'll want to focus on one at a time. Targeting several markets at once can often feel like running several different businesses simultaneously.

I recently consulted with a friend who had started a new business and made the classic mistake of targeting several different markets all at once. I advised him to pick one industry or market and master it. Build your reputation and revenue quickly in one before adding others, I told him.

Creating a reputation for your business in a vertical market takes time. Digital marketing methods may make it easier in some respects, but that's a double-edged sword. Because it's easy to create a digital presence, most markets have become cluttered with marketing-message overload. Unless you have a large staff that can do the work for you, tackle one vertical market at a time. Ideally, it's a market that's large enough for you to commit to for a long time.

With all this said, a firm with multiple reps/advisors/consultants can certainly hit multiple target markets if each person selects their own niche. That's what one printing company I consulted with did with its 11 reps. I've helped several banks and insurance companies do this, too.

3 Strategies for Maximizing Your Target Market

Now, let's focus on three strategies to help you maximize your results in your target market. This is all about creating a reputation that leads to new clients.

1. **Position yourself as a specialist.**

   When you talk about your value proposition in a way that demonstrates that you're a specialist in your target market, you are more likely to catch someone's attention. Which opening statement do you think is more likely to create interest and curiosity about your value?

   I work with small business owners who want to grow and protect their wealth. OR

   I specialize in working with owners and executives in the printing industry who want to grow and protect their wealth.

   Another word you could use is "expert." "I'm an expert in . . ." or "My expertise is . . ." I know that some people have difficulty calling themselves an "expert." While I believe this thinking limits you, I appreciate that you do need to be able to choose words that roll off your tongue with ease and confidence. Perhaps focusing on building a portfolio of clients in that niche will help give you the necessary confidence to claim the "specialist" or "expert" label.

2. **Meet the influencers.**

   Every target or niche market has Influencers. They might include association presidents (past, present, and future) and members of the association's board of directors, as well as the more successful and/or respected industry members.

   To maximize your target market, you must find ways to serve them. How you do this can be related to or totally unrelated to your core business. For instance, you might be able to assist with their philanthropic interests? Be careful not to come on too strong about the business side of things, though. Serve first. Be interested in them. They will then turn their attention back to you once you've built trust.

3. **Speak, write, start a podcast, get interviewed, and get quoted.** Most experts who have achieved a reputation within a target market have writing and speaking in their strategic plan. You establish yourself as a "thought leader" by writing for and speaking to your target market.

   You might write articles for an association newsletter, trade magazines, or your blog dedicated to the target market. You might speak at association chapter meetings or educational events you host. Once you've truly established yourself as someone who "leads the discussion" related to your area of expertise, the market's media will seek you out for interviews. Other experts in your target market will start quoting you, too.

   Don't like to write? Record your thoughts using a smartphone recording app or another device, get the recording transcribed, and hire an editor to turn it into a blog post or article. Don't like to speak? Take a course. Join Toastmasters.

Markets Are People, Too

Your target market might be an industry, but never forget that markets are made up of people. Even in a business-to-business (B2B) sale, you are selling to individuals and committees.

You don't market to an industry; you don't market to a company. You market to *people* in that industry and company. As you formulate your value proposition and marketing plans, always think on two levels: the industry or market segment and the decision-makers you need to reach.

Likewise, you must focus on two levels of problems or opportunities: macro (industry or company) and micro (the individual). The more knowledgeable you become about your target market, the better you will understand and be able to leverage how the macro problems and opportunities impact the individuals. This will make it possible for your messaging to address both levels at the same time.

In a B2B-focused business, your target market may be an industry facing certain challenges or opportunities. You certainly want to address those in your messaging. You also want to take on the challenges and opportunities of the specific individuals with whom you are communicating.

For example, maybe you have a solution that can save the company thousands of dollars by making a production process more efficient. The entire company will benefit from it. Even so, there are usually several people attached to that problem who have their own needs and aspirations that can take priority over the corporate goal. If you only speak to the corporate problem and ignore the individuals involved in solving it, your value proposition's effectiveness will be severely handicapped.

Let's say your target in a business-to-consumer (B2C)-focused industry is pregnant women. That's a pretty narrow focus, right? But these days, that focus isn't usually narrow enough. Are these women lower, middle, or upper income? Are their buying decisions affected by their geographic location, age, marital status, due date? How about if it's their first pregnancy—or not? You can see how the more you know about your target, the better you'll be able to reach them effectively.

RADICALLY RELEVANT ACTION STEPS

1. Look at your client base. What target market do you already have brewing with your current clients that you can leverage?
2. Meet with a few clients in this potential target market who have some affinity for marketing. Let them know you're thinking about focusing on other people or businesses like theirs. Ask them, "If you were working to establish a reputation in this market, how would you go about that? Who would you try to meet and with what groups or meetings would you get involved?"

"When you try to appeal to everyone, you run the risk of appealing to no one."

—Bill Cates

RADICAL RULE OF RELEVANCE #5

Only differences that matter, matter. Why is your differentiation important and/or valuable to your clients? What is the benefit that your distinction brings to your clients?

CHAPTER 7

Solve the Right Problems

You must be able to identify and solve your ideal prospects' biggest problems. How you do that is important to your business and how you communicate your value. When you can show empathy for their challenges, help them see how those challenges impact them, and position yourself as someone who can help, you will be seen as a highly relevant and credible resource. They simply can't afford to ignore you.

In this chapter, you will gain an expanded perspective on how to position yourself and your company as the solution to your prospects' problems.

Identify the Villain in the Story

Every now and then, I run across a book that falls into the category of, "Darn. I wish I had written this book!" Allow me to introduce you to one that is well worth your investment of time and a few dollars: *Building Your Story Brand* by Donald Miller.

As my company was adjusting its branding and messaging, our entire team went through Miller's process and found it extremely helpful. With

Miller's permission, I will take you through one small (but significant) part of his process as it relates to the critical topic of identifying the problems you solve for your ideal clients.

First, just a bit of context. As the title suggests, Miller puts his ideas in the framework of stories, often using movie examples. He says that most successful movies have three principle characters: the hero, villain, and guide. In the early *Star Wars* movies, Luke Skywalker was our hero, Darth Vader was the villain, and Yoda was the guide. Miller says you want to position yourself as the guide. That allows your prospects and clients to be the heroes of their stories.

This is key, because too many people selling a product or service try to set themselves up as the hero. They confuse establishing their credibility with making themselves the star. They focus on themselves too soon in the "story."

Using the principles of radical relevance properly, you want to become so targeted in your marketing message that your prospects see themselves in the story you tell and the examples you provide. They see that they can move from problem to solution with your guidance.

In *Building Your Story Brand*, Miller helps the reader learn how to talk about their prospects' and clients' problems using the same tools that screenwriters use. One of them is the hero's conflict with the villain. As I go through Miller's model, I'll show you how I used this for my own business. Then I'll offer a few examples from some of my consulting clients.

The Villain

The villain is something external to you and your business. Barriers that keep you from reaching ideal prospects are common villains in your story, as well as mine. These might be marketing-message overload, the Do Not Call Registry, and gatekeepers, to name only a few.

While the villain is the antagonist who causes the hero serious problems, the villain is also the catalyst to the hero's growth. When there's no problem to overcome, there's less chance for growth.

As you think in terms of using the problems you solve to gain your ideal prospects' attention, be sure to address both external and internal problems when communicating your value.

To orient your messaging to address your prospects' and clients' problems, the first step is to determine their *external problems*—such as barriers to saving money for retirement, difficulty positioning their business to sell it, keeping track of changing government regulations, etc.

Internal problems tend to be the emotions people experience because of the external problem. These include frustration, self-doubt, anxiety, fear, denial, and intimidation. Miller makes a good case that someone's "internal desire to resolve a frustration is a greater motivator than their desire to solve an external problem."

B2C and B2B

This concept of external and internal problems works equally well in both B2C and B2B scenarios. Remember, businesses are made up of people. The more you can determine the external and internal problems your prospects experience, the more effectively you'll gain their interest and earn their business.

When you're speaking with corporate contacts, discuss how company problems are affecting them personally. Discover the impact of the problem on both the company and them.

This chart presents examples of external problems that cause internal problems. Notice how most of the internal problems come down to a few common emotions.

Industry	Clients' External Problem	Clients' Internal Problem
	Their self-talk	*How they are feeling*
Commercial banker's prospects and clients	"How do I get the best interest rate?" "Can I qualify for a large enough loan?"	Confusion, worry, fear
Financial planner's prospects and clients	"There's so much conflicting information coming at me all the time."	Confusion, anxiety, denial, inaction
Real estate agent's prospects and clients	"I'm not sure who I can trust to make sure I get the best deal possible."	Worry, slow to take action
Business consultant	"I have to get my company to be more profitable . . . soon!"	Anxiety, fear, doubt, stress

Ask Questions

Quite often, the best way to elicit both types of problems is to ask questions that demonstrate how well you already know a bit about their world. The tighter your target market, the more you can make a few educated guesses. Looking at their LinkedIn or Facebook profiles can often be helpful. Of course, the best way to learn about a prospect's world is to get introduced to them by someone who knows them fairly well.

Here's an example of a statement that opens up into a question: "It's pretty common for folks to feel inundated and even a bit confused by the sheer volume of conflicting information that comes from different sources. Are you experiencing that, too?"

Asking the right questions can help you create instant resonance. I vividly remember a phone call where a prospect's response to my question was, "Were you a fly on the wall at our leadership meeting this morning?"

To be able to create relevant and compelling messaging, it's critical for you to know both the external and internal problems faced by your prospects and clients.

One of my financial advisor coaching clients, James, puts it this way: "There are a lot of deep, negative feelings surrounding the topics we discuss most often with people, including death, incapacity, getting old and not being able to care for yourself, or running out of money in retirement. Those feelings cause many prospects to be in denial about the problems. I've found that by simply asking the prospect if they can relate to this dynamic opens them up—they see that I *know* them, which demonstrates empathy which, in turn, increases trust."

How Do You *Fit Into* Their *Story?*

Marketing consultant Lee Bradshaw (www.one27consulting.com) rightly observes that one reason prospects might ignore your message is because you're making it about *you* instead of about *them*. Bradshaw says, "They don't care about your story as much as they care about how you fit into their story. If your website, marketing material, etc. are full of words describing how amazing your company is, then people are tuning you out, and you are losing money."

He cautions against leading with how great your company is or how many awards you have won. Instead, he says, position yourself as someone who understands them. Show them that you're someone they can trust. You don't do this by focusing on you and how long you've been in business.

Stand Out by Solving the Big Problems

There's no question in my mind that communicating how you solve key problems for your target market is the most critical part of creating a relevant and compelling value proposition.

Working as a venture capitalist and founder of Start Up Secrets (www.StartUpSecrets.com), Michael Skok has witnessed many businesses climb to the highest heights of success, then go down in flames. He has an interesting perspective on problem-solving that I hope you find useful. When we talked for this book, he asked me, "What is the number one reason businesses fail?" Feeling confident, I replied, "Not being clear on their target market."

His response was, "No, that's usually reason number two. Try again." Slightly less confidently, I guessed, "Not clear on the problems they solve."

"Yes," Skok replied! (Whew! It only took me two tries.)

He explained that they often either aren't clear on the main problem they solve, or the problem they do solve might not be big enough to sustain a successful business. Another way to phrase this would be the problem needs to be important enough to the prospect for the individual to invest their time and money to solve (or prevent) it.

You probably solve multiple problems for your clients. As you develop how you communicate your value, consider that a large percentage of your marketing message should focus on the biggest, most obvious, and most urgent problem your target market faces. I'm not saying that you don't discuss the other problems you're able to solve. Just start with the biggest and/or more prevalent one, and then bring up the other problems as appropriate.

As I reflected further on Skok's comments, I knew he was right. In my 25 years of helping businesses grow and thrive, I'd say that the reason many businesses underperform is that they aren't crystal clear on the problems they solve coupled with not having a laser-focused target. Most small businesses and professionals try to be too many things to too many people. This dilutes their value messaging.

About an hour after my conversation with Skok, I decided to look as smart as he is. Over lunch with a colleague (let's call him George) I asked, "What problems do you solve?" His first response was, "I provide consulting and coaching to business owners and their sales teams." George didn't answer my question, did he? He described what he does, but not the problems he solves. If I asked *you* this simple question, how would you answer?

Gently letting George know that he didn't really answer my question, I asked the question again. This time he said, "I help businesses with complex sales simplify their methods and messages so they win more clients." Better, but he still didn't state the problem.

The main problem for George's target clients is client acquisition—attracting and converting more high-level clients. A couple of related sub-problems are: sales taking too long to convert and sales being less profitable. The reason for these problems is that businesses with complex sales tend to create complicated processes and messaging that adds to the complexity and confusion. Humans crave clarity, and a confused mind doesn't take action. Your prospects want to be crystal clear on the problem(s) you solve and crystal clear on the steps they need to take in order to work with you.

The solution that George brings is a framework that simplifies the entire sales process, so the prospect and sales rep are always clear on where they are in the sales courtship and what still needs to be accomplished. The net result is that George is helping his clients get faster yeses and faster nos. This moves more prospects through their pipeline more quickly, which increases sales and profits.

And the Problem Is?

I first became acquainted with Skok through an article he wrote for about what he calls, "The 4Us." With his permission, I'll quote and paraphrase what he shared in this article. I've added B2C scenarios where he only shared B2B applications. (Italics are direct quotes from Skok.)

He writes: *A significant part of defining a value proposition involves what I like to call the 4Us. If you find yourself answering a definitive yes to the majority of these questions, then you are on the right path toward a compelling value proposition. If not, consider re-evaluating and revising your new venture.*

Here are his "U" questions.

Is the problem Unworkable?

B2B: *Does your solution fix a broken business process where there are real, measurable consequences to inaction? Will someone get fired if the issue is not addressed? If the answer is yes—then that person will likely be your internal champion.*

B2C: If the problem is not fixed, are there real and measurable consequences for inaction? For example, if someone has a problem with the IRS breathing down their neck, they typically want immediate relief and will pay for it.

Is fixing the problem Unavoidable?

B2B: *Is it driven by a mandate with implications associated with governance or regulatory control? For example, is it driven by a fundamental requirement for accounting or compliance? If the answer is yes—then that group will likely be a champion.*

B2C: Is the problem driven or influenced by government regulations? For example, currently in the U.S., an individual must start taking distributions from their retirement plan by age 70.5. Many people will benefit from professional advice on how to take those distributions and balance that money with other sources of income. This is an "unavoidable problem."

Is the problem Urgent?

B2B: *Is it one of the top few priorities for a company? In selling to enterprises, you'll find it hard to command the attention and resources to get a deal done if you fall below this line. If the answer is yes—then you know you'll have the attention of the C-suite.*

B2C: What is a top priority for an individual client/customer, and is there a time frame associated with it? You have a rodent problem? Get rid of them today! (Get rid of them yesterday, in fact!)

Is the problem Underserved?

B2B: *Is there a conspicuous absence of valid solutions to the problem you're looking to solve? Focus on the white space in a market or segment. If the answer is yes—then you know the market is primed for the solution.*

B2C: It can be difficult to find a problem that nobody else is attempting to solve, but maybe you can solve it better, faster, or more completely.

What about Opportunities?

As mentioned in Chapter 3, cognitive neuroscience has taught us that human beings have three primary motivators: solving problems, optimizing opportunities, and completing tasks.

At the risk of being overly simplistic, your prospects' amygdala (sometimes referred to as the "reptilian brain" or "old brain") is on the lookout for danger and problems. Is the situation safe? Do I trust? Do I run?

Your prospects' prefrontal cortex ("higher brain" or "new brain") goes to work to evaluate, generate feelings, and make decisions about what action to take. If there is no threat that needs to be dealt with immediately, it turns its attention to: Is there an opportunity? Is there a reward I can achieve?

As you might guess, all of this happens very quickly. The amygdala scans its environment up to six times per second, while the prefrontal cortex scans at a rate of about two times per second.

So what does all this mean? It confirms what most people have known intuitively for a long time—finding, fixing, and preventing problems is usually a more powerful sales and marketing tool than finding and maximizing opportunities.

This is why I led this section with problems and challenges. I believe that generally speaking (there are always exceptions), your messaging should start with pointing out, empathizing with, and offering solutions to your prospects' problems or challenges.

Don't Ignore the Opportunities and Rewards

Personally, I like to lead with the problems I solve and/or prevent and then discuss the opportunities I can help my clients realize.

At first blush, some products and services may appear to focus solely on the opportunity. For example, I like using the Tunity app, which scans a television screen, recognizes the network and the show (or event), and then streams the audio to my smartphone. I use it at a bar or restaurant where a sporting event is being shown without sound and when I want to listen to the news while doing various things around the house.

When I first learned about it, my reaction was opportunity-based. "Wow! Now, I can listen to the game in a noisy environment!" But this opportunity didn't exist without the problem: You can't hear the game in bars and restaurants.

So here's the grand conclusion: Build your value messaging to include both the problems and the opportunities. You never know which will resonate more with your prospect. Empathize with their problems and challenges, and then show them the full upside or opportunities that await them once their problem is fixed and their challenge is solved.

RADICALLY RELEVANT ACTION STEPS

1. Identify the top three (biggest) problems you solve for clients. Then, break them down into external and internal problem categories.
2. Compare these top three problems with Michael Skok's "4 Us." Do these big problems contain at least half of these characteristics? If not, you may want to go after more important problems for your clients.
3. Look at the opportunities you provide to clients. Is the opportunity based on an underlying problem? If so, perhaps you should build your message on both the problem and the opportunity.

"Companies tend to sell solutions to external problems, but people buy the solutions to internal problems."

—Donald Miller

RADICAL RULE OF RELEVANCE #6

Differentiation for differentiation sake is worthless.

The goal of creating differentiation is to create both perceived and real value to your prospects and clients.

CHAPTER 8

Hit the Bullseye

In shooting sports, the bullseye almost always wins you the most points. In business, hitting the bullseye almost always wins you the most profitable revenue. Radical relevance is all about hitting the bullseye.

The best way to introduce this chapter is with an example I heard from the brilliant Phil M. Jones in his Audible Original, *How to Persuade and Get Paid* (https://adbl.co/2Z40ffW). Jones asks us to imagine what we would do if we were in a shopping mall and lost track of our children. While I never truly lost my daughter in a mall, I did experience the momentary panic of losing sight of her on more than one occasion. And while I don't want to trivialize the terrifying circumstance of a missing child, the critical nature of this scenario works to emphasize the importance of getting your bullseye right.

Says Jones, "Knowing you must find the children, how well would you describe them to a stranger to increase your chances of finding them? You'd give them everything, wouldn't you? Hair color. Eye color. Height. What they were wearing. You might reach for a picture you were holding on to. . . . You know that the better the description, the more likely people will be able to help you find your child."

He explains that you'd share that picture with people who have "leverage"—security and anyone else who could influence your ability to find your child. This is what we do with missing people.

This applies to "missing clients," too. If you would like to find more Right-Fit Clients, the first thing you have to do is decide exactly who they are.

This is what I mean by hitting your bullseye.

Getting to the Bullseye

The bullseye in your target is clarity about your Right-Fit Client. As mentioned earlier, a Right-Fit Client is one that is perfect for you because you are perfect for them. Right-Fit prospects (destined to become your clients) will resonate immediately with your message. Right-Fit prospects will say to themselves, "Finally! Someone who gets me!"

If you found yourself in a meeting of expert marketers, you would probably hear the word "persona." The best marketers know that a target market is made up of individuals. Whether you work B2B or B2C (or both), you're always trying to communicate your value in a way that will resonate with the human beings who make up your market—the more specific the better.

Persona is a fancy word for ideal client, or in my parlance, Right-Fit Client. Don't get confused by this new terminology. The point is that you want to develop and use a crystal-clear picture of your ideal client—the type of person you are trying to attract into your world. An ideal client is a Right-Fit Client.

The term persona was first introduced and popularized in the marketing world in Alan Cooper's influential 1998 book, *The Inmates Are Running the Asylum*. He defined personas as representatives of real people—"hypothetical archetypes of actual users." They're based on research into your target—a target you come to know so well that you can add a name and personal details.

Adele Revella writes, "In the simplest terms, buyer personas are examples of archetypes of real buyers that allow marketers to craft strategies to promote products and services to the people who might buy them."

Persona Marketing is More Relevant Marketing

Jake Wagner, principal at Wagner Communication Systems and host of the podcast *DigitalMarketing4fp* (www.DigitalMarketing4fp.com), works with financial advisors. He explains the concept this way: "You probably have defined your ideal clients' age, income, and profession. Identifying your target market is a worthwhile exercise. At the end of the day, though, you're attracting human beings, not target markets. . . . Target markets result in a shallow understanding of who you're trying to find." We must go deeper.

Let's say an accounting and consulting firm wants to do more work for small business owners and has decided to find one or more target markets with which they can go narrow—to understand the prospects more deeply. Here is a simple illustration of what that process might look like.

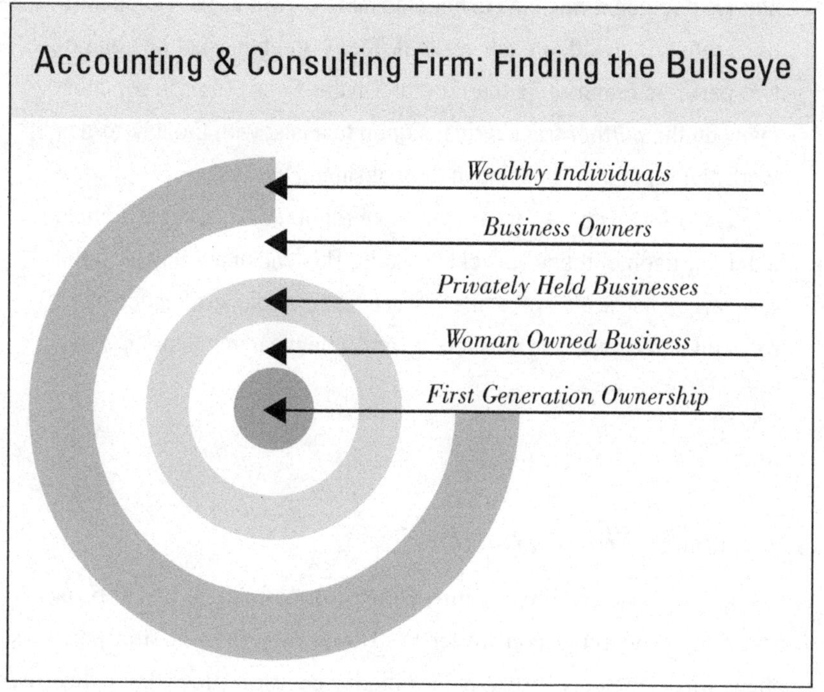

Figure 4

ONE FIRM—MULTIPLE TARGET MARKETS

Founded in 1927, Snyder Cohn (www.SnyderCohn.com) is an award-winning, mid-sized CPA and business advisory firm serving business owners, executives, and nonprofit organizations in the Washington, D.C. metro area. Clients range in size from start-ups to organizations with revenues in the hundreds of millions of dollars.

The firm has developed expertise in several vertical markets that include real estate development companies, medical practices, nonprofit organizations, hospitality businesses, and tech startups. These vertical markets developed over time—more organically than by design—due to the firm partners' experience, proclivities, and relationships.

When I was brought in to help the company grow more intentionally, we decided it was time to become more proactive with each partner's reputation within each vertical. Today, each market has one or two partners featured as the face of Snyder Cohn. Their associates, many on the partner track, are assigned to assist with the day-to-day work and reputation-building in their assigned vertical.

As I write this book, we are putting a reputation-marketing plan in place for each of these vertical markets. This will allow Snyder Cohn to leverage its varied areas of expertise and interest, craft much more relevant and compelling messaging, and achieve much faster growth.

Get Inside Their Head

Says Wagner, "You need to get into your prospect's head. It will be easier to find your prospect if you understand how they tick." Using personas will help you identify your Right-Fit Clients' decision processes, concerns, barriers, opportunities, and fears, as well as where they congregate and get their news, the organizations they join, and other key demographic and psychographic details. Going back to Miller's storytelling approach, you learn their story and how you, as their guide, can help them become a hero in their own story.

Revella says, "You'll learn that buyer persona research ensures that your marketing addresses your buyer's perception of the problem, not the founder, CEO, product manager, or public relations agency staffer's perception. This builds a bond of trust with your buyers that leads them to quickly see that you have the ideal solution for them, making your salespeople's work easier and quicker."

The more you develop and communicate your value proposition based on your crystal-clear persona, the more your messaging will resonate with them. This increased empathy and resonance will lead to more interest on their part. They will think, "This guy gets me" and "Finally, someone understands me."

The combination of a clear target, a highly focused bullseye, and paying attention to some tactical relevance (covered in Part 3), guarantees you will hit the bullseye in their brain. Hitting that target will result in catching the attention of just the right prospects for you, setting more appointments, and converting more clients.

Personas Make for More Effective Marketing Initiatives

I recently consulted with a product-based business that was sending marketing emails to warm prospects—people who had requested information. When we began working together, their email open rate was about 17 percent, which allowed them to be profitable, but not thriving.

I quickly noticed that most of their marketing message was about the product—the features and benefits. That was *their* story, not their *prospects'* story. So I had them adjust their messaging to be more focused on their prospects' challenges, problems, opportunities, etc. Their open rate jumped to 36 percent. I had to remind them that they chose their target market because their product was perfectly suited to that audience. Their mistake—which is all too common—is that they didn't laser-focus their messaging to make it radically relevant and critically compelling.

Figure 5 lists some of the attributes to take into account as you create your buyer persona.

Identify Your Personas for Your Right-Fit Clients

DEMOGRAPHICS (SUCH AS)

- Age
- Gender
- Location
- Income
- Title
- Where they congregate

PSYCHOGRAPHICS (SUCH AS)

- Fears/Anxieties
- Goals/Opportunities
- Attitudes
- Buying style
- Responsibilities

Figure 5

Figure 6 provides one of the ways you can define your bullseye. Some marketers will even give their personas names.

Edward Entrepreneur

Medical Device Research and Manufacturing

COMPANY
- 20 years
- 180 employees
- 2 locations
- Sole owner

BACKGROUND
- Age 58
- Married / Grown Children
- College degree
- Sold 2 previous businesses

MOTIVATORS
- Loves building businesses
- Loves growing his people
- Wants to do good in the world
- Wants to leave a legacy

BEHAVIORS
- Works long hours
- Current with technology
- Well-known & networked in his industry

FRUSTRATIONS
- Would like more free time
- His money isn't working hard enough

HOW WE CAN HELP
Personal CFO & Financial Quarterback

Figure 6

Persona Buyer Insights

Too many people responsible for developing marketing messaging confuse a prospect's demographic profile with a persona. The demographics are just the beginning of creating your persona, because they don't tell your Right-Fit prospect's story. Demographics don't provide much in the way of the true insights you need to craft and deliver the most relevant and compelling messaging.

In addition to the demographics, you need buying insights, which tell you how buyers think about the decision you want to influence. About this, Revella notes, "A person's thoughts about an impulsive or low-consideration buying decision usually reside in the realm of the unconscious. Conversely, a high-consideration buying decision involves, by definition, considerable conscious thought that can be expressed, evaluated, and analyzed."

Shall I translate that for you? The decision process your next client goes through is likely a high-consideration process. They may do some of their own research before even contacting you. They may interview more than one service provider—looking for the right fit for them. And they will certainly place high value on you being recommended by someone they trust. So because the decision to work with you is a high-consideration process for your Right-Fit prospects, you want to learn about their buying process journey and use that when creating and communicating your value.

The insights you gain from talking to prospects and clients about the journey they took to reach you can be tremendously valuable. When you know their journey, you know what concepts, phrases, and words to use because you will be echoing what they have told you. You will be speaking their language. You will be resonating with the bullseye in their brain.

The 5 Rings of Buying Insight

In *Buyer Personas*, Revella presents five types of insight about the journey your Right-Fit Clients take to find you. When you have conversations with prospects as they enter your world and with current clients to learn how they came into your world, certain patterns related to the actions they took to connect with you will emerge.

Since every business is different, I can't tell you what these insights will be for your business. Sorry, but you'll have to do the work. I suggest you identify 10 to 20 current Right-Fit Clients and ask them about the insights I'm about to share from the book. Then, as you continue to bring prospects into your world, ask them these questions as a part of your courtship process. Their answers will give you awareness and understanding of who that person sitting in front of you truly is, while showing you what that person and your defined target "persona" have in common.

Why is this important? Because how you message your value—be it on your website, in your emails, or even during your appointments—needs to be informed by the insights you gain.

So with Revella's permission, here are her "5 Rings of Buying Insight," along with some of my commentary.

Insight 1: Priority Initiative

This insight explains the most compelling reason that buyers decide to invest in a solution similar to the one you offer, and why others are content with the status quo. In Chapter 20, I discuss the dynamic of a problem going from being aspirational (nice to solve) to critical (must be solved).If the problem is perceived as critical, someone will invest time and dollars to fix the problem.

Insight 2: Success Factors

This is what your persona perceives as a successful solution and/or a successful relationship. Not what *you* consider successful, but what *they* consider as such. This is a conversation about expectations. What does success look like for them in achieving their goal?

Insight 3: Perceived Barriers

What's getting in the way of fixing their problem or maximizing an opportunity? These barriers might be people. They might be market or industry conditions. Barriers can also be their own mindset. Once you know their perceived barriers, you can position yourself (or your firm) as someone who helps remove those specific barriers. You might also know about barriers they haven't yet considered. When you share your insight and prescience with prospects, you set yourself up as an expert who has seen this before and knows the best path forward.

Insight 4: Buyer's Journey

What work did they do that led them to you? What research did they do? Have they spoken with colleagues, associates, or friends? Have they spoken with one or more of your competitors (or are they planning to do so)? Ask them about this before your first meeting. You need context for their journey before going into your "pitch." Imagine how you might tailor your approach if you know they've already met with competitors versus knowing that they haven't yet but are planning to do so.

Insight 5: Decision Criteria

While the other four insights lean toward the bigger picture, this insight starts to get more granular. You want to learn which questions they asked as they evaluated alternate ways to solve their problem. What did they want to learn as they visited different websites or consulted with peers? Which details in the collateral material helped or hindered their decisions? Your goal is to learn which attributes of your product or service spoke to them. Revella says, "Decision criteria insights frequently surprise marketers by revealing that buyers are not satisfied with benefits-oriented marketing materials, and that companies that communicate facts are more likely to gain their buyer's trust. You may even learn that your newest or most distinctive capabilities have the least impact on their decision."

This last statement by Revella isn't to suggest that benefit-oriented messaging is unimportant to your prospects. It's the mix of how you describe your offering's features, advantages, and benefits that will impact your persona.

For example, I am consulting with a successful financial advisor targeting physicians. He said that first and foremost, most physicians are process-driven. They don't just want to know that you can help them. They want to know *how* you're going to do that. What is your process? Knowing the advisor has a well-defined process gives prospects the reassurance they need.

The point is that we can never assume what we think will work. We must give our prospects and clients a seat at the table. Literally!

Finding Ideal Prospects Gets Easier

I am not a good fisherman, but even so, I used to take my daughter out to nearby ponds, lakes, and rivers to teach her how to do it. I even took her to a pond that I heard had been re-stocked the day before. My friend told me that the fish were practically fighting over his hook. For me and my daughter? No luck! With this knowledge, you know why I hesitate to offer up the trite but true advice, "Fish where the fish are." But it's still valid advice.

Your persona is most likely a member of one or more affinity groups, both in person and online. And as sites such as Facebook and LinkedIn have become robust search engines, it has become increasingly easier to narrow your searches to find those who come very close to matching your personas while excluding those who don't. Your messaging resonates instantly with those you connect and, therefore, grabs their attention. Your marketing time and dollars are most efficient.

Know Your Persona's Why

In other parts of this book, I discuss the importance of having one or more client-focused whys. This refers to *why* you believe in your value. It may be similar to your company's mission.

It should go without saying, but I'll say it anyway—your client-focused why should be perfectly aligned with your persona's primary challenges and/or aspirations. The clearer you become about your persona so you can then orient your why to their problems, challenges, and opportunities, the more powerful your why will be. There will be a natural resonance between you and your Right-Fit Clients.

When you humanize your message and share why you believe in your value (which is often accompanied by a short story), you give your prospects and clients permission to share *their* why. Over time, this dynamic begins to peel back layers of the onion so you learn more and more about your clients. This puts you in a position to serve them better and create deeper engagement that leads to steadfast loyalty and referrals.

One of the smartest things you can do to grow your business is to determine why your clients decide to work with you. Knowing their fears, needs, and wants is part of this. Once you figure this out, you can begin to spot trends and common denominators that you can use to improve your marketing messaging. In fact, you'll be able to articulate what they feel, but can't quite express.

No More Than 3 Primary Personas

Can you have more than one persona? Of course. From a tactical standpoint, if you have two or three personas who are likely to land on the homepage of your website, you can have graphics and text that represent each persona. Each visitor can click on the link that's most relevant to them.

I do that with my website. My three primary personas are:

- **Individuals/professionals** interested in how we can help them acquire more Right-Fit Clients through relationship marketing strategies.
- **Leaders/corporate** individuals looking for ways to help their representatives be more effective with business development. They also want to increase revenue without increasing their marketing budget.

- **Meeting professionals/leaders** looking for a sales speaker who can deliver a high-content, dynamic, and even fun presentation. (That would be me.)

You'll see those three personas identified prominently on our home page at www.ReferralCoach.com. Click on the right option for you, and you'll go to the information that's most relevant to you.

Developing Your Personas

Creating your essential buyer personas will take time and research. Start by interviewing the right people.

"Who should I interview?" I'm glad you asked. Start internally with your salespeople, marketers, product development staff, and client service staff. These are people who will have a handle on client needs and expectations.

But don't stop there because the input you gain from internal sources is biased by their own roles. Be sure to also talk to as many real buyers as you can. For B2B, that might be people on the buying committee. For B2C, go right to the consumer with focus groups, surveys, and other means. Include people who chose not to buy from you to learn why.

In addition, study analyst reports, industry-specific reports, LinkedIn profiles and groups, social networks, industry portals, job descriptions, and other relevant sources of information.

Do this with three categories: Past customers, recently acquired new customers, and prospects who didn't buy from you. Getting three different insights will help you better tailor your messaging for each group since what you communicate to win back a former client might not be the same as what you direct to a current customer.

The Most Fundamental Mistake

You should never, ever, ever, ever develop and communicate your value proposition, marketing messages, and the like without bringing current and prospective clients into the conversation. Writes Adele Revella, author of *Buyer Personas*, "The fundamental mistake I see people make is that they are attempting to build buyer-focused messaging in a setting where the buyer's perspective is unrepresented."

Without speaking with real prospects, we run the risk of using confusing jargon or words and phrases we like to use (that we think are clever and effective) rather than those that resonate.

The message development process needs to take the company's goals into account for sure, but it must also include your buyer's perspective and needs. Even when your product has benefits or features that will help your prospect, if those benefits/features aren't on their radar yet, you must back up and start by addressing your prospect's primary concerns first.

Revella writes, "Your decision is simple: Effective messaging emerges at the intersection of what your buyers want to hear and what you want to say."

Show Them You Know Them

One lesson I learned long ago is that no one will ever have the context a business owner has about their business. I first learned to be careful about this with my employees. Even after 40 years of running my own businesses, I have to constantly tell myself, "Bill, your team members will never have the context that you do. Slow down. Provide the context for your decisions."

Guess what? The same is true about context for prospects and clients. They have their own context—their fears, problems, challenges, priorities, goals, and opportunities—that you'll never completely have. But you must work to learn these as best you can. Similarly, they will never have the context you have about the value of your work—the knowledge, experience, wisdom, products, and services you bring and the results you can create for them.

There are two levels for this context learning:

1. **Strategic:** Your persona, being the amalgamation of your Right-Fit Clients, is on the level I term "strategic relevance." This is important context, but still a bit abstract, since your persona is only a representation of your Right-Fit Client.
2. **Tactical:** Before reaching out to a living, breathing prospect, you need to gain as much context as possible. Keep doing it during contact with them to test assumptions and modify messaging as needed to remain relevant.

This is why you must know your Right-Fit Clients as well as you possibly can. The time you invest and the work you do to truly know prospects and clients is what will distinguish you in the marketplace. It's what will allow you to look different and cut through the noise, grab attention, and convey the messages needed to convert prospects into clients. Everyone asks, "What makes you different?" Clever phrases can help, but the real distinction is created from the work you do to know your clients and to show that you know them.

RADICALLY RELEVANT ACTION STEPS

1. Create one to three primary personas for your Right-Fit Clients. (For assistance, check out the resources in your Radical Relevance Toolkit, www.RadicalRelevanceToolkit.com.)
2. Make sure your client-focused why (why you believe in your value) is aligned with your Right-Fit Clients' why. Your value needs to match what they need.
3. Share your client-focused why with prospects early in your new relationships and with current clients who may not have heard it yet.

"It's not a coincidence when it feels like a company's marketing message and content was created especially for you. It means a marketer somewhere did his or her job well. It means that they took the time to understand their buyer's goals, needs, and objections."

—David Meerman Scott

PART 3

Tactical Relevance

Now it's time to get tactical. In PART 3, we'll examine how you can turn those strategic decisions into real actions. Tactical relevance decisions show up everywhere you communicate your value, including:

- Website headlines
- Website text
- LinkedIn profiles
- Email subject lines
- Email messages
- Social media posts
- Questions you ask
- Videos
- Blog posts
- Podcasts
- Articles, reports, guides, and whitepapers
- How you answer your phone
- How you ask for referrals
- Anywhere and everywhere you communicate your message

Let's take a deep look into how you can start to craft some of your messaging.

RADICAL RULE OF RELEVANCE #7

Market to people. An industry and a company are made up of people. Market to the people in that industry and company.

CHAPTER 9

The Foundation of Your Message

I wrote this book to address the common challenge many businesses face: How to craft a message that hits the bullseye in their prospects' brains. It's a message that will attract the right prospects, repel the wrong ones, and move both to whatever action you recommend.

In this chapter, we begin the nitty-gritty process of creating your message. For most, this isn't an easy process. When I help business owners and business development professionals do this in workshops, I warn them, "Don't be surprised if your brain starts to hurt. For most, this is not an easy process, but I'm here to make it easier for you."

8 Foundational Questions

Your messaging begins by asking yourself some foundational questions. I've adapted the questions below from those used by the established pro at helping financial advisors communicate (and price) their value, Leo Pusateri of Pusateri Consulting (www.PusateriConsulting.com).

Before reading them, imagine you are sitting face-to-face with the biggest prospect you've ever met—your dream client. That person grills you with one question after another, expecting you to answer quickly, clearly, and confidently. If you can't, you'll be dismissed to make room for others vying for the business.

Without thinking, answer these questions about your company quickly:

1. What do you do?
2. How do you do it?
3. Who do you serve the best?
4. How do your clients usually benefit?
5. What is your experience producing these results (benefits)?
6. What makes you different from all the others trying to gain my business?
7. Why do you do what you do?
8. Why are you right for me?

So how did you do? Did you have short, clear, confident answers? If not, you may be using too many words and trite phrases to describe your value. Work on it, because every prospect and center of influence needs these questions answered to do business with you or to introduce you to potential clients.

You probably won't have to cover all of these questions in one meeting, but if someone asks you any one of them, you'd better have an answer. And if you're reaching out to new prospects through any medium, be it voice, email, or LinkedIn, you will want to address a few of these questions quickly and relevantly to spark their interest and earn a few more moments of their coveted time.

You also want to address them in your website's "About" section.

I'll go deeper into your answers to these questions later in this section, but first, a few thoughts about the content that goes into your answers.

5 Critical Message Elements

If you want to communicate your value proposition effectively, always keep these five critical elements in mind as you craft your answers to the eight questions above:

1. **Clear and Concise.** Your answers must be free from industry jargon and complicated sentence structure. Keep them to one or two sentences. One notable exception will be your answer to, "Why do you do what you do?" Because your "why" usually involves a brief story, this may range from 10 to 20 sentences. (And, yes, in general, you can have different versions and lengths.)

2. **Conversational.** You're talking to a person, not submitting a high school English class essay. Speak and/or write informally, while still following the basic rules of grammar.

3. **Client Benefit-Oriented.** Try to think beyond features and advantages to the benefits that will resonate with clients. For instance, how long you've been in business is not a benefit. Turning a feature into a benefit usually requires saying something like, "Which means to you . . . ." or "So therefore . . . ."

4. **Convey Emotion.** People mostly make the decision to work with you or refer you to others based on how they feel about you. Yes, your value needs to be there as well, but if they don't like and trust you, you're going nowhere. Support this process with emotional words such as safe, secure, fear, confidence, risk, dreams, mistake, turnover, profit, commitment, loyalty, and gap when you can.

5. **Cite Examples.** This brings your value proposition to life. An inventory of examples allows you to tailor what you say to each

audience in a way that creates maximum relevance. Note, however, that using examples they can't relate to can work against you. For example, if you mention large corporate clients to a small business owner or solopreneur, you will create a disconnect. Your example will be irrelevant!

Not every response to these foundational questions needs to include all five of these critical message elements. That would be unwieldy and work against keeping them concise. Just do your best to incorporate as many as you can and in different ways. (I'll provide a formula for this in a following chapter.)

DON'T BE ALL THINGS TO ALL PEOPLE

Like many youngsters, Todd McDonald made extra money cutting the neighbors' lawns. He later turned this into a real business, expanding his services to include driveway resurfacing. He was making good money, but he had always been interested in finance—insurance and investments—so he made a shift in his career that put him on a path to remarkable success.

As a freshly minted financial advisor, Todd visited with several industry veterans, asking them what would turn out to be a life-changing question: "If you could start your business over, what would you do differently?"

Almost everyone commented, "I would not try to be all things to all people. I would pick a target market."

Todd took this advice to heart and eventually settled on a target market that had tremendous upside and fit his experience—family-owned, closely-held, heavy construction companies. His clients build roads, bridges, airport runways, and commercial buildings.

The messaging on his company's website is designed to resonate with his Right-Fit Clients by using certain keywords such as "insider's understanding" and "achieve independence," as follows: "We combine our insider's understanding of the construction industry with our experience helping family-owned and closely held businesses with business succession, employee retention, and estate tax minimization."

His company, Broadstone Advisors (www.BroadstoneAdvisors.com), has established a national reputation in his selected target market.

Move Away from Irrelevance

Business-to-business marketing strategist Ardath Albee (www.MarketingInteractions.com) recommends moving away from irrelevance by replacing "we" and "our" with "you" and "yours." Because many of us (you) don't work for brands that command instant attention, we (you) need to work harder and be more conscious of how we (you) construct our (your) messages and conversations based on who we're (you're) talking to.

For example, while writing this book, in my effort to demonstrate that we (you and I) are all in this shift to radical relevance together, my tendency was to use "we" and "our." However, that makes my message to you a bit less personal. This may seem like a subtle concept, but it's actually quite profound. Any distance I create between me, the creator of my message, and you, the recipient, lessens the message's impact.

Irrelevance in Action

To find irrelevance in your communications, Albee recommends starting with your website's "About" page. Is the emphasis on you or your clients? Even a few misplaced words can skew the meaning. Here are a few examples:

- *We are committed to providing a level of service to our clients that makes us a leader in our industry.* Notice how this sentence conveys that the company is more concerned with being seen as a leader in their industry than in serving its clients.
- *We are focused first and foremost on creating long-lasting client partnerships by collaborating with them to identify their needs and provide solutions that support their success.* Notice in this sentence how the client becomes front and center in the message simply by replacing *their* with *our.*

A simple shift in the emphasis placement will draw the reader into the message (personal), rather than creating distance (impersonal).

Albee points out that one of your biggest challenges is getting out of your own way when creating messaging about products and services you know better than anyone else. Each time you create content, ask yourself, "So what? Why should my client care about this? What is the clear benefit to my client of what I'm creating?"

When you get good at this, your customer obsession becomes clear. As Albee writes in her book, *Digital Relevance* (www.marketinginteractions.com), "Customer obsession is based on deep knowledge, insights, and context that enable marketers to intuitively align the distinct value their company provides at the intersection of what their customers need. When marketers become customer-obsessed, they become naturally oriented toward aligning their messaging and programs with their buyers' context." Rather than thinking about how to promote products, think first and foremost about how you can enable your clients to find higher levels of success.

Should You Ditch the Pitch?

As you probably already know, the elevator pitch concept teaches that you need to have a short and clear way to communicate your value. If someone asks, "What do you do?", you want to have a concise and clear answer.

I have nothing against elevator pitches. I've just made the case for the fact that everyone needs a short and clear way to communicate their value. I have observed, however, that how people learn to create their elevator pitch doesn't produce authentic or effective messaging. Professionals, business owners, and salespeople are instructed to catch someone's attention with cute phrases that often work against clarity and credibility.

For example, I once heard a financial advisor answer the question, "What do you do?" by saying that he was a "financial nutritionist." Clever? Perhaps. Clear and credible? Nope!

To distance myself from the cheesy versions of the elevator pitch, I'm using the term "value positioning statement." In the next chapter, I'll help you craft one that's highly relevant.

RADICALLY RELEVANT ACTION STEPS

1. Write down your answers to the "8 Foundational Questions," keeping them as short as possible.
2. Then, rework your answers with the "5 Critical Message Elements" in mind. You may not get all five elements into each answer, but try for more than one.
3. To refine even further, put these answers away for a few days and revisit them with fresh eyes.

RADICAL RULE OF RELEVANCE #8

Think solutions and benefits before promotion.

Before you promote your solutions, first focus on the transformation your offer creates for your clients. Spend 70 percent discussing the transformation and 30 percent on how you'll make that happen.

CHAPTER 10

Your Value Positioning Statement

Let's get super tactical and think of the exact words you want to use to describe what you do. Your value positioning statement (VPS) will serve you well in many situations. Think of it as an elevator pitch 2.0.

The words you chose for your VPS are important because words resonate in the brains of your prospects and clients. People immediately add their own meaning to words you use. This dynamic can work for or against you.

The more you know about your target market in general and your persona(s), the more likely you are to choose the right words. Your choices must also be authentic for you. This is important. Otherwise, you risk coming across as awkward and uncomfortable, and your language won't match other aspects of your brand (and personality).

With all that said, sometimes you don't know much about the other person, such as a first-time visitor to your website or LinkedIn profile. Therefore, you also want to craft a few generic statements you can use when you're not certain who's receiving the message.

The Miracle VPS Formula™

Here's a formula for communicating your value that allows you to incorporate all or most of the eight foundational questions from the last chapter in just a few short sentences. That's why I call it a miracle formula. It's efficient and effective. I've been using and teaching it for years. I use it both in written and oral communication.

By filling in the blanks, you'll create your ideal message. Here's a quick overview before we take a deeper dive into the language you'll use.

1. My/Our expertise is in ______________________________.
2. I/We work with______________________________.
3. Who want to______________________________.
4. For example, ______________________________.

Let's look at this more closely. I'll start by defining each step in the formula and then provide a few examples that will help you create your own. After that, I'll challenge you to get to work on this for you and your business. We have some tools in our Radical Relevance Toolkit at www.RadicalRelevanceToolkit.com that will help with this as well.

Step #1: My expertise is ____________________ .

If you introduce yourself with your industry label—financial advisor, insurance agent, accountant, business consultant, investment banker, attorney, etc.—the person you're addressing will immediately assign their own meaning to those words. Is this good or bad? That depends on their history with that job title.

For example, if they worked with a financial advisor who they felt was self-serving, expensive, or unethical, the mere mention of those words will create a negative response. You may not observe it, but it's there. Can you overcome that? Sometimes.

This same dynamic can be ascribed to just about any label you might use. An effective alternative is to use the words expert or specialist.

The dictionary defines "expert" as: *a person who has a comprehensive and authoritative knowledge of or skill in a particular area.* Isn't this you?

The dictionary defines "specialist" as: *a person who concentrates primarily on a particular subject or activity; a person highly skilled in a specific and restricted field.*

Again, isn't this you?

Therefore, when speaking about what you do—whether answering a query or volunteering a statement—consider saying, "My expertise is in ____________" or "I'm a specialist in the area of ________________."

Who is respected and usually gets paid more in our society? Is it a generalist, or is it an expert or specialist? You know the answer. Stating your expertise or specialization allows you to talk about what you do with confidence, but without appearing arrogant.

Step #2: I work with ______________________________ .

This step defines your target market. Can you have more than one target market? Yes! Can your target market be broken up into even more narrowly defined groups? Of course! But in this step, don't mention more than two target markets (one is better).

You want to make this as specific as you can and still be relevant to anyone you want to attract into your world. Remember, the more general, the less impactful. Since relevance is derived from context, the specific situation at hand will dictate how narrow you can be. For example, how you state this on your website and LinkedIn profile might be a bit more general than when you hit the bullseye for a specific prospect, client, or strategic alliance.

Step #3: Who want to ______________________ .

One of the five critical message elements from the previous chapter is "be client benefit-oriented." Here's where you incorporate that. When you speak in terms of what your Right-Fit Clients want, you'll be stating a clear benefit. For example, a financial planner is often addressing the prevalent fear of running out of money in retirement. So a financial planner might want to say, "I work with individuals who don't want to run out of money in retirement."

You'll recall that the fourth of the five critical message elements is to convey emotion. Just about any time money is involved, emotion is close at hand. The example above—"I work with individuals who don't want to run out of money in retirement"—evokes emotion in the recipient.

On the B2B side, let's say you're an investment banker. You might say, "I work with business owners who want to exit their business knowing their employees will be well taken care of and their legacy will remain in place."

An accounting firm targeting a specific market might say, "We work with non-profit organizations that want to put tight financial tracking and reporting in place to enable better strategic decisions."

Step #4: For example . . .

While steps 1, 2, and 3 get things started, the full picture will likely need just a little bit of help from what I call "value in action." (This term actually came from one of my clients, Chris Kolenda, as we worked on his VPS.) By providing an example that's totally relevant to your message recipient, you will fill in the gaps and bring your value positioning statement to life.

Your value in action statement could be a real-world example (a very short story), your client-focused why, a key point of differentiation, or how you create results. And, yes, humor is allowed if it fits with your personality.

This formula is designed so that if it's used in writing—say, on a website, in promotional literature, or in an email—the reader quickly gets a clear sense of what you do. And if you use this formula verbally, the same goal is accomplished, leading to a more in-depth conversation. You may hear, "That sounds great. How do you do that?"

It might help to look at a few examples. In each, the "for example" piece is the value in action.

Example #1: My business, Referral Coach International

My expertise is in business development for professional service firms.

We work with individuals and their firms . . .

Who want to acquire more high-level clients and increase their revenue without increasing their marketing budget.

For example, we helped a Canadian company use our system to go from 100 clients to more than 1,000 in seven years. We are now working together on an ambitious goal to double its clients over the next three years.

Example #2: Financial advisor

My firm specializes in financial planning and financial management.

We work with owners of fast-paced businesses . . .

Who want a financial quarterback to make sure all aspects of their financial life remain in perfect shape.

For example, most successful business owners are laser-focused on achieving their business goals but don't devote the time needed to create and manage a plan that will help them achieve their personal financial goals. So as their financial quarterback, we pull together the perfect team to make sure they have the right insurance in place, a benefits package that helps them retain their best employees, and all their investments working hard for them.

Example #3: Commercial banker

My expertise is in business banking.

We work with business owners in the manufacturing sector . . .

Who want to thrive in this climate of unpredictable and constant change.

For example, we're different from most banks. While any bank can provide financing at a competitive rate, we are more than just a lender. We strive to become a valuable resource to you in many areas of your business by applying our knowledge, experience, and support before, during, and after any project. We've been working with one small manufacturing business for 10 years that now sees us as a true business partner. Its management doesn't make a move in the business without checking with us.

Example #4: Business consultant

My expertise is in reviving businesses whose growth has stalled.

We work with business owners . . . .

Who want to breathe new life into their businesses so they grow more quickly and profitably.

For example, I've built and sold three businesses. Each one of them went through a lull in growth. The experience of jumpstarting each company has led me to develop a proprietary formula that can be applied to virtually any business. I enjoy seeing a struggling business owner get excited about his or her business again. I believe that I'm doing what I was meant to do.

Variations on Step #1

In helping hundreds of businesses develop their messaging, I know that leading with "My expertise is . . ." doesn't fit all businesses and personalities. So here are a couple of variations I've seen many people use effectively to begin their message.

1. **Ask a question that draws them in.**
   When you just can't seem to bring yourself to openly acknowledging your expertise, you might find this variation worth considering. It's particularly helpful when you're in face-to-face situations.
   Ask a question that will help put a frame around the work you do and draw the other party into your answer. The question usually takes the form of, "You know how most people (or businesses) . . ."
   You know how most people face retirement concerned about running out of money? I work with . . . who want to . . . .
   You know how most CEOs wonder if everyone around them is sharing their most pressing concerns and best ideas? I work with . . . who want to . . . .
   Have you noticed that most business owners seem to complain that their business owns them? I work with . . . who want to . . . .
   I think you get the idea. Play around with this a little. What question might you ask that could draw the listener into the rest of your message?

2. **Make a bold statement that grabs their attention.**
   When working with my clients to help craft their VPS, I've heard some bold or fun statements from time to time that are worth considering as your Step #1. They capture attention—never a bad thing. The rest of the VPS needs to relate directly to that first statement and bring clarity and life to it. Here are three real-life examples:

- *I help my clients create indestructible wealth!*
- *I'm a mortgage specialist, but I feel more like a marriage counselor.*
- *My expertise is in making your biggest and most difficult business challenges go away forever.*

What About Social Settings?

How you describe your value usually needs to be adjusted to fit the context. For example, what you say on your website will vary slightly from how you might explain it to a prospect or to someone you meet at a business networking event. Likewise, how you answer the proverbial what-do-you-do question in a social setting will have to be different from what you'd say in a business setting.

Imagine you're sitting around the Thanksgiving dinner table, and a relative you only see once a year asks, "What is it again that you do?" If you whip out your well-rehearsed elevator pitch, their response will likely be, "That's interesting. Please pass the stuffing."

The challenge in social settings is to describe what you do in a way the helps people think of you when a friend or colleague talks about specific issues that fit your expertise. Prospects, as well as clients and centers of influence, will think of you when they see you as a credible resource for solving specific problems. Conversation triggers can help.

Julie Littlechild, co-host of the "Becoming Referable" podcast (www.becomingreferable.com) that I enjoy and recommend, told me a story about "conversation triggers" that helps put this idea in context.

"I was at a conference where one financial advisor described his value by saying, 'We are wealth and life builders. We provide investment management services and financial counsel to individuals, families, and organizations.' It was well-crafted, but here's the problem. I have never been at a dinner party—or any other social event for that matter—when someone said, 'You know what I really need? I need a wealth and life builder who can provide me with investment management services and financial counsel,'" she said.

For social situations, Littlechild believes you want to move beyond the value proposition and craft stories that help people understand the problems you solve. She recommends focusing on conversation triggers—words or phrases you use to describe the problems you solve. They match how people actually talk about those problems. When you use the same words others use, you help them connect the dots in their minds.

Here's an example for a financial planner. Consider these possible conversation triggers:

- "We keep arguing about money."
- "I feel like I have to make all the decisions."
- "We just don't seem to be on the same page about the future."

The conversation-trigger response might be, "I help couples communicate about money so they are both pulling in the same direction."

When you're talking to someone at a social gathering, you might say, "Here's what we're hearing a lot lately. Many of the couples we work with say they keep arguing about money or they just don't feel like they're on the same page. So a big part of our process is bringing couples together and having a deeper conversation about what they value and how they think about the future. That clarity creates a shared vision. It's amazing how the conflict seems to disappear."

Later, when that person hears any of those trigger words or phrases, they will likely think of you as the solution (and, hopefully, introduce you to the people who need you).

Try This

Littlechild suggests the following exercise:

1. Identify just one of the problems you solve for your clients.
2. Consider what clients might be talking about with friends or family that would suggest they are dealing with that problem. What are the trigger words or phrases?
3. Describe the problem you solve using those trigger words.

For example, one problem a commercial banker solves for his/her clients is helping a cash-strapped business get access to enough capital to scale the business—to put it in position to take advantage of realistic opportunities for rapid growth.

So a few of the trigger words that represent the problem might be *capital, cash, growth, opportunity,* and *scaling the business.* The emotional trigger words might be *frustration, dissatisfaction, distress,* and *complexity.*

With trigger words, you now have a way to talk about the work you do in a more natural manner by using words and concepts that happen in everyday life.

We have a "Value Proposition Generator" in the Radical Relevance Toolkit that I recommend you use for your business. This valuable tool will help you develop all the short and clear value positioning statements you need to talk about your full value proposition, including the Miracle VPS Formula™. Get access at www.RadicalRelevanceToolKit.com

RADICALLY RELEVANT ACTION STEPS

1. Write down several versions of your value positioning statement (and variations, if applicable) using "The Miracle Formula."
2. Set these aside for a couple of days; then, revisit and revise.
3. Show the results to a few clients who are likely to provide helpful feedback. Adjust as needed.
4. Re-read the section on trigger words, and think about how you can put this creative concept to use.

"When you use the right words and phrases with the right prospects in the right situations, the doors open sooner and sales close faster."

—Caryn Kopp, Chief Door Opener, Kopp Consulting

RADICAL RULE OF RELEVANCE #9

Relevance begins with client obsession. Radical relevance starts with your obsession for knowing your prospects and clients better than you previously thought necessary and certainly more than your competition does.

CHAPTER 11

The Right Research Makes Your Pitch Perfect

In order to deliver a relevant message that's guaranteed to grab your prospect's interest, you must first research that individual and company. In fact, you should never, ever, ever contact a prospect without doing even a little research. After all, how can you deliver a relevant message if you don't have much context about who you're contacting?

There are two primary research categories you can tap into before contacting your new prospect. Both have value.

Cold Research

With cold research, you're not talking to people to get information. You're mostly using online research to learn about both the prospect and, if applicable, the prospect's business. Cold research includes, but is not limited to:

1. Reviewing the company website and their profile if it's available.
2. Reviewing the prospect's LinkedIn page.

3. Googling them. You can often find articles and press releases written by or about your prospect.

Sam Richter (www.SamRichter.com), author of *Take the Cold Out of Cold Calling*, is one of my favorite resources on this topic. I recommend looking at his proprietary *Sales Intel Search Engine* (https://www.sellingintel.com/a/cates) as one of your sales research tools.

Warm Research

This type lets you learn certain kinds of information that you aren't likely to get with cold research. It involves finding out what you can from people who know your prospect, especially your referral source. Here are some questions to ask:

1. **What's going on in their life (and/or business, and/or career) that's most important to them right now?**
   If you can position the introduction (and your follow-up) to them in a way that ties the work you do to what's top of mind for them, you now have a radically relevant approach. You will at least gain their attention.

2. **Can you give me a sense of their personality?**
   This will help determine how you might adjust your communication style to be more in line with theirs. Are you dealing with someone who's bottom line-focused or open and chatty? Can you bring some humor to your approach?

3. **How do you think they'll react to this introduction?**
   Do your referral source and this person regularly exchange resources and make introductions? Is the prospect typically open or resistant to new ideas?

4. **Tell me something you like, admire, or respect about them.** This is one of my favorites because I can usually find a way to apply what I learn to my approach—and I'll bet you can, too. For example, your referral source might say, "She's an extraordinary networker. She seems to know everyone, and everyone knows her." When you reach out, you can say, "George said that one of the things he admires about you is your ability to network. He told me that you are one of the best he's ever seen." There's nothing wrong with leading off with a little flattery.

Not Limited to Referrals and Introductions

Warm and cold research should not be limited to approaching prospects for your business. You can research anyone before connecting with them. Doing so will give you more confidence when meeting new people while helping to generate more meaningful conversations.

For example, let's say you're going to a philanthropic event that will include some heavy hitters with whom you'd like to connect. Research in advance everyone you hope to meet—just enough to learn a few things about each. It's amazing how much more confident you will feel in approaching these "strangers" and how much further your conversations will go when you're able to bring relevant topics to them.

RADICALLY RELEVANT ACTION STEPS

1. Identify the information you wish to learn about your new prospects through research tools such as Google, LinkedIn, and YouTube (cold research).
2. Identify the information you want to learn about your new prospects from your referral source (warm research).
3. Make it a habit to always do research before you contact prospects so you increase the probability of hitting them with the right message, at the right time, in the right way.

"Research creates relevance. Relevance is irresistible."

—Bill Cates

CHAPTER 12

Creating Your Differentiation Gap

Relevance can often come from what differentiates your business from others, but many people struggle to determine and communicate what makes them different from their competition.

Differentiation is developed through strategy and implemented through tactics. This chapter demonstrates how you can identify and use your differentiation on a very tactical level.

The Gap Method of Sales Messaging

Chief Door Opener Caryn Kopp (www.koppconsultingusa.com), author of *Biz Dev Done Right: Demystifying the Sales Process and Achieving the Results You Want*, uses what she calls The Kopp Gap Method of Sales MessagingSM. It's an amazingly simple formula that allows you to identify (or create, if necessary) a differentiation that separates you from your competition without saying negative things about them. Here's her formula:

Anybody can ____.

Not everyone can ____________________________________.

For example, ____.

This formula is designed to get the other person thinking, "Huh, I never thought about it that way. We need to have a meeting."

Essentially, you want to generate enough separation and/or curiosity on their part to continue the conversation with you and agree to the next step, whatever that might be. And as with just about all the other formulas, templates, word tracks, and scripts that I provide in this book and companion online toolkit, the actual wording you use will vary from situation to situation and person to person. As Kopp puts it, "Sales messaging is situational. It's really important that you consider the specific situation, your relationship to the prospect, and other factors that might compel you to adjust to be more relevant for your prospect."

Bringing the Gap Method to Life

Kopp works with businesses to open doors at the highest levels in an organization. Here's how she applies her formula when speaking about her own business:

> *Anyone can say they can get a couple of meetings for you or do some lead generation, but not everyone has a 20-year history of getting C-suite and executive-level meetings on behalf of their clients to discuss large engagements. For example, one of our clients added $7.3 million of incremental revenue (so far) coming from 168 meetings over the course of four years, which resulted in 55 new clients.*

"We express it that way because there are a lot of lead generation companies. What I need to do when I'm speaking with someone is create that gap of differentiation. I need to do it to level the playing field with competitors in a way that shows we add value. This will help get the right prospects to talk to us," Kopp says.

In addition to creating that differentiation, the gap formula acknowledges that you understand that your prospect is probably being contacted by a lot of people. When I sold printing many years ago, I'd reach a buyer on the phone and say, "I know you get a lot of calls from people selling printing. I'm just curious, am I the first or the tenth today?" Almost everyone I called would laugh at that question.

Whatever their answer, I would reply with, "When the others call, what do you tell them?" I'd get another laugh. The humor would eliminate any knee-jerk reaction they might have and open them up to a productive conversation. They appreciated the fact that I understood their challenge of having to fight off or sift through all the potential resources.

Kopp offered another example involving a company in the promotional products industry. She challenged the salespeople to think about what was truly different about their value.

"The truth is, nobody really cares why you're different," she says. "They only care about how you offer more value. When I asked this client, 'Why would a prospect find more value with you?', the response was, 'Oh, well, we have great customer service."

Kopp pointed out that great customer service was entry level—it was expected. She pushed the client to articulate a value that was so significant that prospects would make time on their calendars for a meeting. With that in mind, the president talked about a situation where production problems delayed work on a client job, but once things were back on track, the company chartered a plane to fly the merchandise so it would arrive on time.

Here's the differentiation that came from that story: While anybody can say they believe in customer service, not everyone would charter a plane to get the order to the client on time. Bam! This "value in action" can create an image in someone's mind—they can visualize a plane with their order racing to them.

Here's the sales gap message that emerged from this story: *Any company can say they provide great service, but only we will go to extreme lengths to make sure our customers are thrilled. For example, we knew a customer needed an order to arrive in time for a conference. We chartered a private plane to make sure that happened.*

Kopp recommends that when working on your messaging surrounding the gap—the differentiation—leave yourself a voicemail with your message. Putting yourself in the shoes of a decision-maker, listen to your voicemail message. How is it coming through? If you were that person, would you clear time on your calendar for a meeting? If the answer is "no," or you're not sure, then you are not done with the message. Keep going.

Expanding on this, I would add:

1. Not only do you want to put yourself in their shoes (as best you can), take your thinking to some of your clients for their feedback. They have context that you don't have. They will take what you say and tell you what it means to them. This process almost always results in a better message.
2. If you bring value through a specific process—if you have a three-step or a seven-step process that creates value—name that process. When you give it a name that no one else uses, you have instant differentiation. You're the only one with that process!

The message you create using Kopp's formula can work in just about any format used to convey your value: voicemail, conversation with a prospect, at a networking function, an email, on your website, in your LinkedIn profile, and any other collateral material you produce.

Be Careful About the Names You Drop

There may be times when you need to communicate a more generic point of differentiation or example of how you're different, though in this world of radical relevance, generic is almost never as effective as specific.

People who approach me with their services often say things like,

"We've worked with _____," which is a large, well-known company. Impressive? I suppose. Relevant to me? Nope. I work with big companies, too, but I'm not one.

This name-dropping approach creates an immediate disconnect. I'm left wondering if they understand the needs, issues, and budgets of smaller businesses. So be careful about the names you drop because you may unintentionally push prospects away.

If you feel you must mention clients that are large companies, be certain to quickly communicate that you understand what's involved in working with a business the size of the prospect you've approached. And give an example to bring it to life—to show your value in action.

Kopp referenced this, too, during our conversation, saying, "It used to be that we talked about messaging with respect to customization. Now we talk about it with respect to personalization. High-level decision-makers want to know that the people who are reaching out to them have done their research and that they've already done the thinking as to why it makes sense to have a conversation. People who skip that step don't get in the door."

RADICALLY RELEVANT ACTION STEPS

1. Use The Kopp Gap Method of Sales Messaging[SM] to develop a few options you can implement in your prospecting efforts.
2. Take these options to a few clients who can discuss what you've developed. Fine tune from there.

"The truth is, nobody really cares why you're different. They only care about how you offer more value."

—Caryn Kopp, Author, Biz Dev Done Right

RADICAL RULE OF RELEVANCE #10

Differentiate between your different "personas." A "persona" is your ideal client profile. Segment your marketing message based on the personas you've identified rather than on your products/services. Apply the right products/services based on which persona you are addressing.

CHAPTER 13

Stop Random Acts of Content

Content marketing has become a major marketing strategy of late because it's an excellent way to make relevant connections with your prospects and clients.

Defined by the Content Marketing Institute (www.ContentMarketingInstitute.com) as, "A strategic marketing approach focused on creating and distributing valuable, relevant, and consistent content to attract and retain a clearly defined audience—and, ultimately, to drive profitable customer action."

Content marketing comes in the form of e-newsletters, e-books, reports, checklists, blogs, white papers, podcasts, and videos.

Although content marketing today is typically in a digital format, it has been around forever in paper form.

One of my earlier books, *Unlimited Referrals*, was published in 1996. (You can probably pick up a copy on eBay for about $3.99.) In addition to selling the book outright, I used it to generate speaking and consulting opportunities. Once someone read the book, they were often interested in how I might help them or their organization implement the strategies and tactics outlined in the book. Using a book, even a printed one, as a lead generator is content marketing.

The Content Marketing Institute notes that most of the information that companies send out isn't very relevant or valuable. "That's what makes content marketing so intriguing in today's environment of thousands of marketing messages per person per day," the organization notes.

I talked to Jay Baer of Convince & Convert (www.convinceandconvert.com) about this because he helps businesses generate purposeful word of mouth, more effective content marketing, and social media marketing that produces results.

"Content marketing success or failure is based almost entirely on relevance," he said, reinforcing the whole point of this book.

With regard to content marketing in email form, Baer said, "We all experience it. We quickly scan our inbox, identify the sender, maybe read the subject line, and sometimes take a quick glance at the content. Then, delete. In less than three seconds, that email was deemed not relevant so now it's gone."

The key to relevancy, he says, is abandoning the notion that the recipient is interested in your message about your product or service.

It's All About Client-Focused Relevance

Ensuring that your content marketing is relevant requires you to truly know your prospects and clients. The only way you can do that is to ask questions. You can automate that process by requiring people to answer a question or two as part of the form they fill out before they can download a report from your website or opt-in to receive email tips. Asking questions in addition to other standard opt-in form information allows you to begin segmenting your email list.

For example, with most of our opt-in forms, we ask the visitor for their first name, email address, and their role. Is the person an individual professional (advisor, consultant, or rep), or are they part of their firm's leadership team (leader, manager, trainer, etc.)?

With this information, we can easily create more relevant messaging for each segment or part of our list. But we don't stop there. We tag each person with a code that tells us what report, checklist, or e-book they requested. We are now able to further tailor our messaging to each segment of our list for maximum relevancy. (Note that the more questions you ask someone in an opt-in form, the less likely the user is to complete the process. It's critical to test what works best for your target market and know that you may have to collect some of the information you want over time rather than immediately).

Baer told me, "The best marketers provide content that tells stories, that injects human elements. They do a better job of delivering something the recipient is willing to engage with, as opposed to yet another weekly product-centric email."

Fair or not, prospects and clients measure and judge the level of client service they receive from you against the best service they have experienced from other (often entirely different) businesses. Likewise, prospects and clients are comparing your ability to create targeted, relevant content to what good marketers are already doing. Generic, overly promotional, or platitude-laden content won't set you apart. Ideal prospects and clients will abandon you for more relevant and compelling content provided by others.

The 3 Cs of Relevancy

In our conversation about content marketing, Baer laid out what he called, "The 3 Cs of Relevancy: Cadence, Content, and CTAs." He is so knowledgeable in this area that speaking with him is like taking a big drink from an information fire hose. Here is a summary of what I gleaned from him.

Cadence

Batch-n-blast (or spray-and-pray), needs to give way to a more sophisticated model for email delivery. Marketing automation allows you to use predetermined rules to decide which recipients should receive what email message. This is particularly effective when the campaign rules are mapped to the customer journey, thus providing increasingly relevant content as the recipient moves through the consideration funnel stages.

Content

Sending the same message to everyone on your list is like expecting everyone who comes into your restaurant to order the same meal. We're individuals, with different tastes, likes, and dislikes. Adding personalization to your email campaign has never been easier, yet it is often still sorely underutilized.

It's more than [First Name]. Personally addressed emails are nice, but pretty much everyone does that, so it's to be expected. More engaging personalization is achieved through ongoing data collection for each recipient, audience segmentation, persona modeling, "nurture rules" based on engagement or lack thereof, and pretty much anything else that can be used to craft a more unique, one-off email message.

CTA (Call to Action)

A call to action is something you want the person who consumes your content to do. Do you want them to download a report? Schedule a phone call with you? Share the information with others? No call to action usually means the relationship that you were enhancing through your content gets put on hold or dies altogether.

Never assume that your content consumers will know what to do next. If you want them to take an action, tell them what action to take.

The True Measure of Effective Content

In his book, *Youtility: Why Smart Marketing Is about Help Not Hype*, Jay Baer writes, "Your marketing should be so useful that people would gladly pay you for it."

He's not suggesting that every piece of content you provide should come with a price tag that requires your prospects and clients to trade their credit card information for that report, checklist, or white paper. This, however, should be one of the standards you use to gauge the value of what you produce.

If you are using some of your content to generate leads or add people to your mailing list, then you will be asking them to pay with at least their email address.

I produce quite a bit of content that clients tell me is useful and valuable. I have an inventory of checklists, videos, and e-guides that I give away with no strings attached. I have another inventory of content that people "pay for" with their email address. These two content engagement paths are designed to lead our prospects and clients to another level of content they will pay for. These are more robust offerings, such as our online video training at www.TheCatesAcademy.com.

You will find that some marketers recommend that in your free content, you should tell prospects *what* and *why* they need to do something. To get the *how*, they need to pay for it. I've always had trouble with this advice. I think that without at least some of the how, many readers may feel a little cheated. So I use a mixture of *what*, *why*, and *how* in the content I create. Is there one right way to do this? Of course not. The right path for you will be determined by the results you produce.

Your Content Marketing Relevance Checklist

Ask yourself these questions about your content marketing's relevance. Refer to this list from time to time as you craft various messages for specific prospects. Note, though, that no message will be able to incorporate all these attributes of a radically relevant and critically compelling message.

Is your message . . .

- ☐ addressing their most blatant and/or critical problem?
- ☐ bringing up an emotional component of their problem?
- ☐ devoid of jargon?
- ☐ devoid of platitudes?
- ☐ crystal clear in meaning?
- ☐ using words your prospects and clients would use?
- ☐ as specific to that individual as possible?
- ☐ demonstrating that you did your pre-message homework?
- ☐ demonstrating why you are a credible resource for them?
- ☐ telling a bit of your client-focused why?
- ☐ being delivered through the right medium?
- ☐ being delivered at the right time?
- ☐ directed at the right person (as much as possible)?
- ☐ creating a sense of urgency or why acting now is important?
- ☐ demonstrating some form of social proof?
- ☐ tapping into the dynamic of loss aversion?
- ☐ providing a clear call to action?

RADICALLY RELEVANT ACTION STEPS

1. Review the content you are producing to provide value to prospects, clients, and alliances. Are you providing a clear call to action so that once someone experiences your content, they will know the next logical step?
2. Explore how you can improve the effectiveness of your content marketing using ideas from the "Content Marketing Relevance Checklist."

"Relevancy creates time, relevancy creates attention, relevancy is the killer app."

—*Jay Baer, Author,* Talk Triggers

RADICAL RULE OF RELEVANCE #11

Know your own client focused "why." Why do you believe in your value? What experiences or shifts in perspectives have you seen that cause you to believe you can bring great value to your clients?

CHAPTER 14

Tactical Relevance With Email

Did you know that engineer Ray Tomlinson sent the first email on June 8, 1971?

Email is still a great way to reach out to a prospect—if and only if—you are able to get the prospect to:

1. Open the message
2. Read the message
3. Respond to the message

It's taken me almost 25 years to perfect a prospecting email formula that produces great results. By the way, I use the verb "perfect" loosely. That's because in the world of sales and marketing, no formula works every time. It's an inexact science.

Personal or Robot?

If location, location, location are the prime rules of retail, then personalization, personalization, personalization are the prime rules of email.

When I work with clients to help them attract more Right-Fit Clients and look at the emails they send, I often ask, "What robot wrote this for you?" If your email even hints at the chance that it's a mass message or an autoresponder, the chances of your prospect opening it are severely diminished.

In today's world, you simply must put in some effort to know a little bit about your prospect before you compose and send your initial email. Personalized will beat out generic every time. (You might find this article on advanced personalization helpful: http://bit.ly/2Odc6Z3.)

Your best source of information is your referral source. But if you failed to get much from them, or you're not working from a referral, do the "cold" research described in Chapter 11.

The All-Important Subject Line

You know how some of the snail mail you receive has text on the envelope to tease you into opening it? The email subject line has a similar primary purpose: to get the recipient to open the message by creating curiosity and showing you know a little about them.

If you have been referred to this prospect by someone they trust, use the referral source's name in the subject line.

Donna—Bob Smith asked me to contact you

Donna—Bob Smith thought we should know each other

Donna—Bob Smith thinks very highly of you

The 5 Parts of the Perfect Email Message

Long emails are easy to write. Crafting a brief, relevant, and compelling email is a lot harder. If you struggle with brevity (as I do at times), ask an associate, friend, or colleague to review your message to find ways to say the same thing with fewer words. Remember, 50 percent of the population will see your email on their mobile phone first. Even a short email on a mobile phone looks like a book.

Each part of the email should be a paragraph consisting of no more than one or two sentences with a space between each paragraph. No dense paragraphs, please! Make the text friendly to the eye, so people will read it (or be able to skim easily).

Part 1: Personalized Opening

Open your message with something that you learned about the prospect and/or their business. This can come from your referral source or other research.

Part 2: Your Value Positioning Statement

I/we work with ______ who want to ________ (and ________).

Part 3: Value in Action

Provide a short example of a success you had with a client with whom they can identify.

Part 4: Call to Action (CTA) with Value Promise

What do you want this person to do? Whatever it is, tell them gently. They can't read your mind. My first CTA is often a request for a brief, 15-minute phone call. I like to tease them with some of the value that will come from that call. I might tell them what other clients are doing that's working for them or that I can send our latest study or e-guide.

Part 5: The P.S.

After your CTA and valediction (a fancy word for your closing or farewell), consider adding a P.S. to reinforce a point or to add an intriguing bit of new information. If someone skims your email first, there's a strong chance they will see and read your P.S. before they read the main message.

When I'm contacting a prospect about a speaking engagement, I'll add my demo video link to the P.S. When the message is about consulting, coaching, or our video-based learning, I'll include a link to information that's relevant to their area of interest.

RADICALLY RELEVANT ACTION STEPS

1. Examine some of your recent marketing-related emails. How have you violated some of the tenets of effective emails laid out in this chapter? What changes will you make moving forward?
2. Go to www.RadicalRelevanceToolkit.com and download the e-guide *Business Building E-Scripts* for ideas on how you can create more effective email and LinkedIn messages.

"One of the most powerful forces in marketing is empathy. *Your prospects want you to know who they are, what they want, and how they feel about their challenges and opportunities."*

—Bill Cates

PART 4

Relevance That Generates Action

It's time to learn how to get prospects and clients to respond favorably to your requests and recommendations so you compel them to move forward. Being relevant is primarily about catching and keeping someone's attention. Being compelling is about moving people to action.

In Chapter 3, you learned about the neuroscience of relevance. I'll begin this section by tapping into my hidden nerd once again and providing a few scientific underpinnings of action, coming at it from several different directions. Knowing the science behind decision-making and action can help you create more compelling reasons why your prospects and clients should act.

After that, we'll take a look at some very specific things you can do with your messages to increase your ability to compel your prospects and clients into following your recommended actions.

RADICAL RULE OF RELEVANCE #12

Know your persona's "why." What motivated them to meet with you? What are the critical problems and/or most coveted opportunities in their life? What motivates them to take action?

CHAPTER 15

The Science of Compelling Action

In Chapter 3, we established that emotion is what compels people to make decisions or take action. Without emotion, no decisions get made. Whenever I say this in one of my speeches, the analytical folks in the room (like my dad) look at me wide-eyed with disbelief.

Are logic and analytical evidence helpful in our decision-making? Of course. But even logic and evidence end up with an emotional reaction. Someone will *trust* their decision or *feel* that they are making the right decision based on their reasoning and evidence.

Cognitive neuroscientist and business psychologist Lynda Shaw told me that because one of the brain's main jobs is to keep us safe and make sure we breed, we wouldn't survive without emotional connections.

"Basically, emotional connections are paramount to our well-being and extremely powerful," she said.

How do you use this to your advantage?

Let's say you make a presentation to a committee. It's designed to get them to retain you for your services. What's the first thing someone on that committee is likely to say? "I like her. I really like what she had to say."

This is an emotional reaction. Of course, they will want to make sure the numbers and other specifics work, but emotions count.

There are a lot of things that can create this emotional response. Let's dig into them.

How Your Prospects and Clients Make Decisions

This is where that cognitive neuroscience we discussed in Chapter 3 comes into play again. Here are the steps:

1. An emotional response is triggered in the amygdala.
2. The emotional response moves to a thinking response in the cerebral cortex.
3. The final decision is a combination of steps 1 and 2 above. The decision *feels* right. They *trust* their decision.

Think of this as a marketing message sandwich—logic and thinking sandwiched between emotion.

In our efforts to market, sell, and influence, the biggest obstacle we face with prospects is inertia. Some prospects are already headed in a certain direction; getting them to adjust course isn't always easy. Likewise, some prospects are stuck doing nothing related to the problems you solve. Perhaps they are in denial, or they see the problems you solve as aspirational rather than critical.

Sir Isaac Newton's First Law of Motion states: *Every object continues in a state of rest, or in a state of motion, in a straight line, at a constant speed, unless it is compelled to change that state by forces exerted upon it.* Say what?

Perhaps you've heard it described this way: *A body in motion will remain in motion, and a body at rest will remain at rest unless acted upon by an outside force.*

In the frictionless environs of space, a satellite will move forward in a constant direction unless it becomes affected by the gravity of a celestial body or one of its thrusters.

Guess what? If you expect your prospects and clients to take action on your recommendations, you may have to become that outside force that grabs their attention and gives them a metaphorical push with a compelling reason to make a change in their current behavior.

Becoming the Outside Force

Neuro-linguistic programming (NLP) teaches a concept called pattern interrupt. Essentially, it means changing someone's pattern of thinking or behaving to get their attention and shift their perspective.

In the context of this book, we can think of pattern interrupt as that outside force you need to become so you can grab someone's attention. Yes, the brain likes to process information that feels familiar because it takes less energy. With that said, sometimes you may need to deliver a message that surprises your prospects and clients—a concept, words, or image they don't expect.

Here are five easy ways you can use this concept in your messaging to capture attention:

1. **Counterintuitive:** I like to say, "Referrals are worthless. Yes—the Referral Coach is telling you that referrals are worthless unless what? Unless you turn them into a great introduction." What can you say that goes against conventional thinking?

2. **Controversial:** Taking a controversial position on a topic related to your business can capture attention. You want to be careful that your position won't turn off your current or future Right-Fit Clients. Imagine if I said to you, "Your business would run just fine without any salespeople." You'd be shocked, wouldn't you? If I followed it up with, "Once you get the referral process

down pat by becoming radically relevant, you won't be selling. You'll almost be taking orders," you'd understand my controversial point.

3. **Creative:** The key is to not let the creativity get in the way of the message. One of my financial advisor coaching clients likes to use the phrase "indestructible wealth." I like it because it's unique. It grabs attention but doesn't confuse. In fact, it will probably garner a smile and the request, "Tell me more."

4. **Startling Statistic:** Statistics can capture attention and draw people into your message:

   - *46 percent of innocent people confess to crimes they didn't commit.*
   - *Only about one-third of the colonists supported the American Revolution at the time.*
   - *60 percent of people can't get through a 10-minute conversation without lying.*

   What statistic related to your business can you use to create interest?

5. **Fun:** If it fits your brand and style, using something fun can interrupt and attract. Look at the plethora of talking animals that businesses use to promote their products or services. A billboard sponsored by a funeral home read, "Text and Drive." (Ouch!) Chevrolet Corvette ran an ad that said, "They don't write songs about Volvos." How can you add a little fun to your messaging?

Remove Their Stress to Get to Yes!

I've done a fair amount of adventure travel in my life—trekking in the Himalayas, reaching the summit of Mt. Kilimanjaro, and camping in the Arctic Circle—to name a few.

In the Arctic Circle, bears were a concern. Imagine for a moment that you're hiking along a trail and come upon a bear who is feeling threatened and looks like he's about to charge you. You have three choices: run, fight, or freeze.

Needless to say, this situation will trigger a stress response—with both neurological and physiological changes in your body.

A cascade of neurological and hormonal activity creates physiological changes to keep you alive (hopefully). Epinephrine is released to increase muscle strength. Glucocorticoids keep you going. Endorphins help you ignore how scary and uncomfortable this feels. (There will be time for that later—presuming you survive.)

Your blood pressure increases, your breathing quickens, and you become more vigilant. Your entire mind and body go through a significant reaction to this threat. For most people, fighting or freezing isn't an option. You will likely run. You will do everything you can to escape this danger.

If you make it back to your vehicle in time, you become immensely grateful. You slowly (very slowly) calm down. You're loving life and everything about it—at least for a while.

But what if the stress trigger were something else entirely? How about the fear of your business failing, losing the most important business contract ever, or leaving a mess for your family behind if you should meet your maker sooner than expected? The stresses your prospects and clients experience are not as easily solved as making it to the vehicle faster than the bear. These are called chronic stressors.

Let's say you create a plan for your client to address the cause of their stress. And while that will provide temporary relief, it may not remove the underlying fear.

When it comes to attracting and winning clients, you put yourself in a powerful position when you can continually address the stressors your clients feel, related to the work you do.

I mentioned above that another option would be to freeze. I equate this to when your prospects and clients go into a state of denial around their problems. Business owners sometimes fail to stay on top of their numbers because they fear their business is on the verge of failure. Many individuals choose to deny the possibility of their death or disability, so they don't purchase proper insurance. This denial is the inertia I spoke about earlier in this chapter.

One of your jobs is to demonstrate to your prospects and clients that standing still is not a good option. You must find ways to compel them into taking action (which is one of the main purposes of the brain).

Clarity Creates Confidence That Leads to Action

You've probably heard the expression, "A confused mind will not buy."

As we discussed in Chapter 3, all human beings—including your prospects and clients—crave clarity. And clarity is associated with survival. The brain's main function is to keep the body alive and to expend as little energy as it can in the process. Our brains continually scan the environment to make sure we are safe. Only when we feel safe can we consider opportunities.

In an article for *Psychology Today* (www.bit.ly/2ZYxN0j), David Rock writes, "A sense of uncertainty about the future generates a strong threat or alert response in your limbic system. Your brain detects something is wrong and your ability to focus on other issues diminishes. Your brain doesn't like uncertainty—it's like a type of pain, something to be avoided. Certainty on the other hand feels rewarding. We tend to steer toward it."

Cognitive Fluency is the Key

Your goal is to eliminate the uncertainty. You can do that with cognitive fluency, which is the ease with which we process information, so we understand what that information means.

Business start-up expert Thomas Oppong wrote that this is important in sales because "If information is made to appear simple, we're more naturally receptive to it. If it appears complex, we're likely to be put off. In general, anything that affects the ease or difficulty of mental processing can—and does—affect people's perception of your brand . . . . If you want to persuade a customer to do something, not only do you need to make that action as easy as possible, but you need to make it look easy, too."

Remember, your prospects' and clients' brains are trying to function efficiently and to expend less energy. Making the brain figure something out takes energy. While there's nothing wrong with being creative, if it gets in the way of clarity, your target may lose interest.

This concept of cognitive fluency applies to a number of things related to how you communicate your value, from the name of your company to the look of your website and how easy it is for someone to do business with you. If the explanation of your value or the instructions you provide are complicated, they will (unconsciously) assume that working with you will be complicated.

For example, according to Oppong, researchers provided participants with specifications for two cordless telephones. One group received telephone specifications that were presented in an easy to read font, the other had specs in a font that was harder to read. When participants in each group were asked to choose a phone, those with material presented in an easy-to-read font deferred their decision only 17 percent of the time, while those with information in the harder-to-read option postponed their choice 41 percent of the time.

The researchers concluded that people viewed their reading difficulty as a clue that the decision itself was difficult to make. That's why it's so important that you pay attention not only to what you say, but how it's presented visually.

But I Can't Make Someone Feel Something

It's true that we can't make anyone feel a specific emotion. An emotional response to stimuli is a very personal thing.

With that said, we sure can influence how someone feels. And the better we know them, the easier it becomes for us to figure out what we need to say to increase the likelihood of eliciting a desired emotion. For example, do you have a loved one who has figured out how to "push your buttons" so that your emotional reaction is almost a foregone conclusion? I suspect you do. (Don't we all?)

The rest of Part 4 is devoted to different strategies and methods you can employ to stimulate just the right emotional reaction that will cause a prospect or client to move forward with your recommended action.

As discussed in Chapter 6, when you narrow your focus to truly understand your ideal prospects—one or more personas—finding the right concepts to use and the right words to express those concepts becomes easier. Narrowing to a tight bullseye gives you the understanding to push just the right buttons of your prospects and clients—to elicit an emotional response that then leads to a decision that's in their best interest. (Sorry! No unethical manipulation allowed!)

Clarity brings a sense of relief, closure, and well-being—and a more relaxed state. The brain loves clarity!

RADICALLY RELEVANT ACTION STEPS

1. Look at some of your marketing messages. Are you making "marketing message sandwiches," where you surround the logical and thoughtful aspects of your message with emotional components that relate directly to fears, problems, and opportunities?
2. Examine ways you can become more of an outside force that shakes up your prospects just enough for them to notice you and want to learn more. What questions can you ask that will get them thinking in new ways and question their status quo?

"Prove what you are saying. Back up your promises with information. Specific facts will tell your story in a believable way."

—Maribeth Kuzmeski, President, Red Zone Marketing

RADICAL RULE OF RELEVANCE #13

Use more personal messaging. Go from impersonal (therefore less relevant) messaging—using words such as *we, our, they,* and *their*—to more personal messaging (relevant) by using words such as *you* and *your.*

CHAPTER 16

Take Them from Here to There

As we just learned, clarity plays a pivotal role in moving anyone to action. If your prospects aren't clear about how to get started with you, they probably won't. Bringing clarity about your core work provides great value. And when your clients are clear on your target and bullseye, they are more likely to provide you with appropriate introductions.

You've probably noticed that one of the underlying themes of this book is how your own clarity about your business allows you to create more clarity in your messaging. Who do you serve? How do clients benefit from your differentiation? Why do you believe in your value and how that applies to clients? A clear, simple, and confident way to express your value, coupled with solid prospect and client knowledge, is a powerful formula for winning new business.

One of the most valuable conversations you can have with a prospect (or client) is about the gap between where they are and where they'd like to be. The process of helping a prospect get clear on what their gap looks like, what it might be costing them (financially or otherwise), and how to close that gap can provide tremendous value even before you begin your formal working relationship.

I learned this simple "here-to-there conversation" strategy from my colleague Bill Whitley of the Risk Advisor Institute (www.RiskAdvisor Institute.com).

I will give you an example of how this process works with a financial planning scenario. It should be very easy for you to translate this process to your specific business.

Step 1: Here

What does your prospect's *here* look like related to the work you do? How about their current financial situation? A financial planner will want to know about a prospect's income, debt, savings, other investments, insurance, and workplace benefits package.

Some people are crystal clear about their *here* and proud that they have stayed on top of their finances. Others have no clue and will appreciate the financial planner's efforts to help them gain clarity.

Step 2: There

This is where the real value starts to kick in. Helping your prospect get super clear about their future—there *there*—is always a worthwhile endeavor.

Dan Sullivan, founder of Strategic Coach (www.strategiccoach.com), has been teaching what he calls "The R-Factor Question" for many years. A generic version goes like this: *If we were meeting three years from today—and you were to look back over those three years—what has to have happened during that period, both personally and professionally, for you to feel happy about your progress?*

Of course, you want to tailor this question to your business and the context of your prospect.

A financial planner might say: *If we were meeting three (or five or 10) years from today—and you were to look back over those three years—what must have happened for you to feel good about your financial situation?*

Be sure to select a timeframe that suits the context.

As with the "here" conversation, some prospects are quite clear on their vision for their future (personal and/or professional). They will appreciate the importance of this question and be proud that they've done the work.

Others, of course, will be clueless, probably not even knowing where to start to figure out their answer. As you might imagine, helping a prospect become crystal clear about their vision for their future can bring huge value.

Remember, humans crave clarity. Clarity creates confidence. Confidence leads to action. After all, how can you remain 100 percent relevant if you don't have a comprehensive sense of their context?

Step 3: Challenges

In some cases, your prospects will know a few of the *challenges* they are likely to encounter on their way to *there*. In many cases, you will know what *challenges* they are likely to face that they haven't yet considered.

In a financial planning context, a *challenge* could be a child with special needs or a workplace benefits package that doesn't optimize their 401(k) contributions.

Step 4: Opportunities

As with *challenges*, your client may know about *opportunities* that might have a significant impact on their planning. You may know of other opportunities from which they might benefit from that they don't know about yet.

Staying with our financial planning example, an *opportunity* that the client would know about could be an eventual inheritance. An *opportunity* they don't know about could be a tax-deferred investment vehicle.

Putting It All Together

The clarity that comes from a here-to-there conversation brings great value to both you and your prospect. The conversation turns into an action plan you and your prospect can begin working on together. The more context you gain about your prospect's situation, the more relevant and compelling your recommendations will be.

RADICALLY RELEVANT ACTION STEPS

1. With your team, identify your business's *here, there, challenges,* and *opportunities.* Then, create a plan to get *there* based on this process.
2. Identify a prospect, client, or ally who will let you practice this process on them. Get their feedback. See how this produces value for them and helps position you to be even more helpful.

"One of the most valuable things you can do for anyone is to help them gain clarity in where they are, where they're going, and how to get there."

—Bill Cates

CHAPTER 17

Let Your Story Move People

I recently asked author and marketer Ardath Albee about her perspective on the relationship between brain functioning and relevance. She immediately brought up the importance of stories and why they work to create relevance, capture attention, and build a relationship.

She told me, "Storytelling is the most powerful method we have for attracting and keeping the attention of others and connecting with them emotionally—whether personally or professionally. It is also the most compelling way to transfer knowledge. Facts are important, but unless they are woven into a compelling narrative, facts are easily forgotten."

Proof of that is neuroscientist Uri Hasson's research using a functional magnetic resonance imaging machine (fMRI) to study the brains of both storytellers and listeners. Hasson learned that a story is the only way to activate parts of the brain that a listener uses to turn the story into their own ideas and experience. Storytelling, then, is the only way to successfully plant ideas into the minds of others.

In addition, Albee explains that our brains produce the stress hormone cortisol during the tense moments in a story and doing so allows us to focus. It also produces oxytocin, the feel-good chemical that promotes connections and empathy during the story's emotional moments. Research even reveals that after watching an emotionally charged movie, viewers had a higher amount of oxytocin, which made them more likely to donate money to a stranger.

Are you old enough to remember *The Go Getter* by Peter Kyne or *The One Minute Manager* and *Who Moved My Cheese* by Spencer Johnson and Kenneth Blanchard? No? How about *The Go Giver* by Bob Burg and John David Mann? These are parable books. All four of them, and others like them, have sold well because the ideas are conveyed through storytelling, which makes them easy to understand.

The classic format of a good story goes like this:

- Hero encounters a challenge
- Hero meets a guide
- Guide provides perspective, wisdom, and a process, and challenges the hero to think and behave differently
- Hero struggles at first and/or encounters more challenges
- Guide continues to help
- Hero grows and is transformed

The Story of Your Why

In Chapter 4, we discussed the importance of sharing your client-focused why—why you believe in your value. This is an effective strategy because there is usually a story behind the why. And as we now know, people listen to stories and facts differently.

Whether you are a business owner or not, you can share with prospects and clients the story of how and why you got involved with your current business. When telling this story, whether written or verbally, be sure to bring your clients into it. Meaning, how does the how and why of your story ultimately provide value to them? Make it relevant to them.

There are many ways you can use your client-focused why to tell a short story. They include why you're still in the business after many years, why you believe your value is more important now than ever before, and why you're with your current firm or employer.

I'm seeing more and more of these stories presented in video format on company websites. One financial planning firm offers a video from every team member conveying their client-focused why.

Your Clients' Stories

Case studies are an age-old way businesses can use the power of storytelling. An interesting and compelling case study will follow the classic story model I just covered. In a case study, your client is the hero, and you and your team are the guides. As noted in an earlier chapter, you want to be careful not to make yourself out as the hero. Every one of your prospects and clients want to be the hero of their own story.

I know that my clients are the heroes, and I'm merely the guide or catalyst with a few good ideas from time to time. Sure, I provide guidance and challenge them, but ultimately, my clients do the work that produces the results and earns them hero status.

Where Do You Use Client Stories?

There's no substitute for a well-told story in person or in a group. I recommend you have two or three versions of your story to fit different time frames. Sometimes you need to be quick, and other times you have the luxury of painting vivid pictures.

Use stories as part of:

- Your website's "about" page
- Blog posts you write for your site or as a guest blogger
- E-books or special reports produced by your firm

- White papers
- A sales page for a product or service
- An email marketing campaign

Company Stories Usually Involve the Why

The most effective business stories usually center around a *why*—like why the founder started his/her company.

For example, when Whatsapp co-founder Jan Koum was young, he couldn't afford to call his father in Ukraine. When his father died before Koum had a chance to see him one last time, he was inspired to create Whatsapp as an affordable and reliable way to communicate. He wanted to make sure everyone could stay in touch globally. At this writing, Whatsapp is valued at US$19 billion.

I guess it's good to have a strong, client-focused why that drives you every day.

A FIRM BUILT ON THE FOUNDER'S "WHY?"

Russ Thornton, a financial advisor for more than 25 years and the founder of Wealthcare for Women (www.WealthCareforWomen.com), helps women who are going through a major life transition deal wisely and powerfully with their money.

While Russ was in college, he watched his mother struggle with her well-being and finances after a divorce.

"She really needed someone in her corner to help her gain the comfort and clarity necessary around her money so she could live a better life. That's why my practice helps women like her do just that," he said.

Russ has chosen a clear target market. His messaging uses language that resonates with his audience. He is attracting Right-Fits Clients™, while not attracting those he's less suited to help.

If you study the company's website, you'll see that Russ has done a masterful job of avoiding financial advisor jargon. Instead, he uses words and concepts that resonate with his prospects and clients.

Here are three examples of Russ's messaging that reflects what his clients are thinking and feeling:

1. *One thing about life is certain: It goes on. Make sure your money does, too.*
2. *Many women ask me, "Am I going to be okay?" Let's work together and make sure you are. For the rest of your life.*
3. *Maybe life has handed you lemons, but you've got the grit and tenacity to make lemonade. Because deep down, despite the huge unexpected changes life has thrown your way, you know you deserve peace of mind.*

Notice how each of these statements elicit an emotional response. Brilliant!

RADICALLY RELEVANT ACTION STEPS

1. Using the classic format of a good story, write one or more case studies where your client is the hero, you are the guide, and there's a results-producing transformation. Start using these case studies in your written and oral value propositions.
2. Create a file that helps you capture the "wins" you help create. Review them periodically so you update your inventory of stories and examples to share at appropriate times.
3. What is the story of your client-focused why? Who was the hero, and who was the guide? What was the transformation? Why did it reinforce your belief in your value?
4. Is your company story different from your personal, client-focused story? If so, work on it so you can communicate it to prospects in written and oral form.

"Your story and why you believe in the value you provide may be your most powerful differentiator. Don't hold back. Tell your story!"

—Bill Cates

CHAPTER 18

The Persuasive Power of Social Proof

Social proof is a marketing term that describes how the actions and attitudes of the people around us influence us, whether what we're seeing is online or in real life. It's the digital world's version of the Good Housekeeping Seal of Approval.

For example, when we see lots of positive reader reviews on Amazon, we are more likely to buy that book than a similar one that has no reviews. The reviews—the "social proof"—tell us that the book has been tested and approved by others. Just like when we get "social cues" about when to laugh in a movie theater from others who laugh, we get a sense of what to buy from the reactions of others.

What does that mean to you? It means that when you demonstrate that others have found value in working with you, prospects are more likely to trust their own decision to work with you. Social proof is something you can point to that says, "See? Others like it, too." When prospects are facing the decision to work with you, seeing that others have made that same decision can be critically helpful.

Social proof—often in the form of testimonials, reviews, endorsements, and content marketing comments and shares—is such a powerful force in marketing that you would be foolish not to find ways to make it work for you.

Seeing that others have taken a certain action moves that action from the unsafe to the safe part of our brain. "Oh—others have done this? They are saying good things? It should be safe for me." This is what happens with referrals and introductions, which are a specific type of social proof.

Influencers and Experts as Social Proof

"Influencer marketing" is a relatively new name for a concept that has been around forever. It refers to how people tend to trust those who are considered experts or opinion leaders. Targeting influencers can help you increase the reach of your marketing messages.

Most information available on influencers focuses on consumer marketing rather than on business-to-business situations. A key difference between the two is that in consumer marketing, the consumers themselves are the influencers, primarily through word-of-mouth communication. In business marketing, influencers are people who impact a buying decision, but may possibly be removed from the actual decision itself. Consultants, analysts, journalists, authors, noted experts, and researchers are examples of business influencers.

Some influencers are paid. While technically this may not be considered social proof, the positive impact on the decision-making process is there just the same.

Sometimes the evidence (which appeals to the logical part of the brain) that comes in the form of social proof is all someone needs to decide (emotional) to move forward with working with you. It helps them trust their decision to work with you.

If you sell services, you are probably emphasizing the relationships you build with your clients. And you should. But when selling an intangible, you are in the evidence business—you need to provide evidence. Social proof is a compelling form of evidence—evidence that speaks to emotions and compels one to take action.

When prospects, clients, or centers of influence hold a neutral view toward you (if that's even possible), then the right social proof—which is a piece of evidence—can move them into seeing you in a more positive light. If they already have a positive impression, then social proof will reinforce and strengthen their perception.

Referrals, Introductions, Testimonials, and More

Referrals and introductions are particularly powerful forms of social proof. Why are they so effective? Because someone who knows your value and likes you has taken the time and energy to introduce you to others they care about.

Of course, the stronger the level of trust between the referral source and the prospect, the more effective this piece of evidence becomes.

Quite often, when someone who has experienced your value recommends you, that's all the social proof or evidence you need. The rest becomes a fait accompli (that's French for "done deal").

To get more unsolicited referrals, learn how to ask for referrals without pushing or begging, and discover how to turn referrals into solid connections from advocates. Grab some of the free resources on my website at www.ReferralCoach.com/resources.

Testimonials: The Kissing Cousin of Referrals

Testimonials are closely related to referrals and introductions because someone your prospects can relate to (the more like your prospects they are, the better) is saying something good about you and your value proposition. Like referrals, testimonials use the concept of borrowed trust.

DISCLAIMER: Many financial professionals are not permitted to use most types of testimonials. The financial services sector of our economy is heavily regulated. Since some bad actors have made false claims over the years, the industry has been compelled to keep things on the "safe side."

For those of you who can use testimonials, my advice is: Don't hold back. These powerful endorsements often speak to the emotional part of decision-making, which we've already established is the more important part.

Here are a few things to consider about using testimonials:

1. Video testimonials are the most powerful because of the energy that comes across in a video. But make these short—20 to 30 seconds.
2. No video? Use the person's photo. The more real and personal you make these, the more impact they will have.
3. If possible, use the person's name, title, company name (if applicable), and location. Again, the more specific you can be with the source, the more effective their testimonial will be.
4. Do your best to make testimonials speak to specific attributes about working with you and/or results you helped produce. If you can't promote financial results, you can still showcase your ability to help clients build clarity and confidence about their situation.
5. Take a proactive approach toward collecting testimonials. Just like referrals and introductions, you can be passive or appropriately proactive. Which do you think will serve you better?

Case Studies

A case study—a problem/solution story—can be a very compelling piece of evidence because it examines the situation in depth. As with testimonials, use real names and photos.

An effective case study should be built on these four cornerstones:

1. The problem and/or opportunity
2. Other related challenges or opportunities that came into play in reaching the desired outcome
3. Actions taken by you, your clients, and others
4. The results and how the client felt about them

Case studies can also be particularly effective when courting centers of influence. Problems solved. Opportunities achieved. These bring your value proposition to light in a powerful way.

Social Event Marketing Employs Social Proof

You can also expand your client base in person by inviting your best-fit prospects to attend social events that you host for a few of your current best-fit clients.

For example, many businesses experience the value in hosting client-appreciation events such as wine tastings, trips to sporting events, or dinners at interesting venues—the options are endless. When your clients who like and trust you get together with other clients who like and trust you, the net result is that they all leave the event liking and trusting you even more.

Create "special invitation events" where the purpose of the event is for your clients to introduce others to you—and that can include potential centers of influence. Seeing your "community" of happy clients may be all the social proof a prospect needs to approach you at the event and say, "I'd like you to look at our situation."

Since social proof speaks to our emotions, it can play a powerful role in your efforts to compel action by prospects and clients.

RADICALLY RELEVANT ACTION STEPS

1. Identify people who would make great influencers for your business. Create a plan for building a mutually beneficial relationship that can lead to referrals, testimonials, and social media posts, shares, and comments.
2. Ask for and use testimonials.
3. Start using client appreciation and special invitation events to get your clients and prospects together.

"The straightest line to relevance with a new prospect is an introduction from someone they already trust."

—Bill Cates

CHAPTER 19

Creating Urgency

When your prospect has a sense of urgency about solving a problem or taking advantage of an opportunity, and they are clear about their path to action, action is inevitable.

If you are the one who reveals an urgent problem and then shows them the clear path to fixing it, you become super relevant. They will choose you.

As we observed previously, neuroscientists and psychologists have been telling us for years that three primary elements motivate human beings to act:

1. Prevent or eliminate a problem
2. Take advantage of an opportunity
3. To complete a task (our brains seem to love checking off the boxes of our to-do lists of life)

Most cognitive neuroscientists agree that preventing or eliminating a problem (pain) is the most powerful of these three. Therefore, most sales trainers will tell you to "go for the pain." Some old-school sales trainers will tell you to "twist the knife until it hurts." I find that rather extreme language, don't you? Nonetheless, an effective and relevant value proposition taps into this important force in our lives.

A sense of urgency will move people to action, especially if the need for a specific result is critically important.

Four Ways to Increase the Sense of Urgency for Action

Here are four ways you can light a fire under your prospects they take action.

1. **Discuss the problem's impact.**
   Whether you uncover a problem by asking great questions, or your prospect is wearing it on their sleeve, you never want to take what they say at face value. There are many ways you might get them to expand on the problem, but the most effective is to have them discuss the problem's impact. In a business-to-business sale, you want to learn the impact on both the organization and the individual.

   For the organization, the impact might be on revenue, profitability, workplace culture, customer satisfaction and/or retention, etc. But don't stop there. The problem is also impacting the individual with whom you're speaking. How are they personally impacted? (And/or how is their boss being affected?)

2. **Address the cost of doing nothing.**
   If your prospect is experiencing a problem or challenge, and you've helped them determine the negative impact on their organization and/or themselves, you can then present your solution. Yes, there is probably a "cost" or "investment" for the solution you provide, but there's also a cost of doing nothing.

I've found that transparency in your process is almost always the best policy. Here is some sample language for you to adapt and adopt:

So from this discussion, we've established that this issue will cost you at least $65,000 in profitability during this calendar year. Yes, there is an investment in our service that will reduce, if not eliminate, these losses. So I think it's a fair question to ask: What's the cost to you of doing nothing to fix this issue?

3. Leverage the scarcity principle.

Using time to create urgency is merely applying the scarce resource principle. Whenever a resource is critical, but scarce, you have urgency. Sports that don't use a time clock still employ scarcity. For baseball, it's innings. Volleyball uses the score. Golf uses the number of holes played.

In some cases, time scarcity might come into play without any effort from you. For example, taxes need to be filed by a certain date, and (at least in the U.S.), individuals must begin taking retirement distributions at a specified age.

You can also apply the scarcity principle to the time you have available or your firm's capacity at certain times.

When my daughter was young, I had to find the right balance between being home with her and traveling for business. I created scarcity by limiting my out-of-town speaking engagements to six per month. When I told clients about this limited availability, it usually spurred them to make a faster decision. I would say, "Just to let you know, I am only able to take six out-of-town engagements per month. I have four booked for the month you're considering, and I'll let you know if any other bookings come through."

When using scarcity in your efforts to move prospects to act, make sure the scarce resource is genuine. If someone senses you are creating artificial scarcity, you might damage the trust you've worked so hard to build.

I often offer one of my highly focused coaching and consulting programs using this concept. Before offering the program, I calculate how much time I have available in my schedule over the coming months and use that to determine how many clients I can take on during that time frame. It's a real number, based on my capacity. When capacity is full, clients must wait until more slots open.

Since action is at the fulcrum of success and failure, time is probably the ultimate scarce resource. How can you apply the scarcity principle to your attempts to move a prospect to act on your recommendations?

4. **Take advantage of loss aversion.**

"Most people are more sensitive to losses than gains of equal magnitude. In other words, the magnitude of our emotional response to losing $100 is greater than the magnitude of the emotional response to gaining $100," writes Preet Banerjee, a management consultant and expert in personal finance (www.PreetBanerjee.com). Some studies have suggested that losses are twice as powerful, psychologically, as gains.

Preet shared a concrete example with me from the world of personal finance. "Loss aversion explains why investors are more anxious about portfolio losses of 5 percent than they are happy about 5 percent gains. The magnitude of the emotional response is greater. One of the most valuable things a financial advisor can do is to know when to reach out to their clients proactively when markets are turbulent. Otherwise, some investors' fight-or-flight response kicks in, leading to short-term thinking that may not be beneficial in the long-term."

The concept of loss aversion tells us that at least some of our messaging should focus on the possibility of a negative outcome if they do nothing or make the wrong decision.

RADICALLY RELEVANT ACTION STEPS

1. Get in the habit of going deeper with the problems you discover. Discuss the impact the problem is having on the organization and/or individual.
2. When you quote a fee or price for a product to fix a prospect's problem, be sure to discuss the cost of doing nothing.
3. Explore opportunities for using the scarcity principle, but make sure the scarcity is authentic—no fake countdown clocks offering a bogus deadline to take action allowed.

"A healthy dose of curiosity will take you a long way in business. Tap into the magic of the phrase, 'Tell me more.'"

—Bill Cates

RADICAL RULE OF RELEVANCE #14

Your prospects and clients demand relevance. Be relevant or be ignored. Be compelling or be forgotten.

CHAPTER 20

Work on Problems That Demand Action

Michael Skok, founder of Start Up Secrets (www.StartUpSecrets.com), has created a brilliant model you can use to determine if the problem you are trying to solve is worthy of your time and attention. It's based on whether prospects and clients will invest their time, energy, and dollars to prevent or fix the problem.

Figure 7 on the following page shows what it looks like and how to use it.

Skok's model places the problem in one of four quadrants comprised of four different terms:

Latent (Hidden): If the problem is latent, then you have some work to do to make the problem known to your prospect or client.

For example, many folks are unaware of the importance of certain types of insurance, such as disability (DI) and long-term care (LTCI). Professionals selling both often find themselves in a long process of discovery and education. They must ask clients gentle, probing questions and provide information along the way to help prospects realize that the problem exists. I often refer to this as "the double sale." First, you must sell the prospect on the fact that there is a problem that must be fixed, then sell them on the idea that you're the one to fix it.

Blatant (Obvious): On the other hand, if the problem is blatant, meaning obvious or easily recognizable, then the prospect is aware of it. You don't have to spend time helping them recognize it. You state the problem; their head starts nodding in agreement. You're at least somewhat relevant. You have their attention. If you discuss that problem's impact and suggest that you might have a fix for it, you will probably retain their interest long enough to make your case for why you should be the one to help.

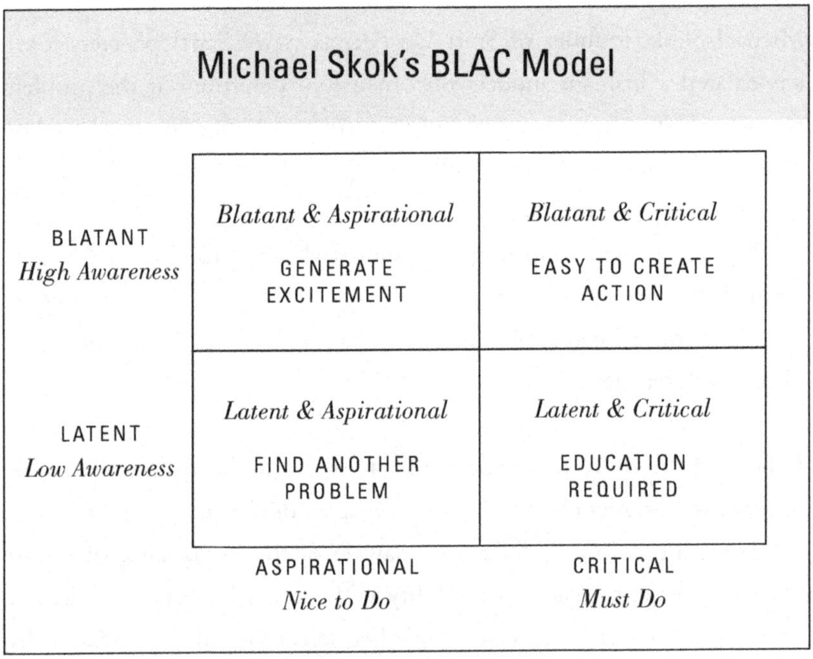

Michael Skok's BLAC Model

BLATANT *High Awareness*	*Blatant & Aspirational* GENERATE EXCITEMENT	*Blatant & Critical* EASY TO CREATE ACTION
LATENT *Low Awareness*	*Latent & Aspirational* FIND ANOTHER PROBLEM	*Latent & Critical* EDUCATION REQUIRED
	ASPIRATIONAL *Nice to Do*	CRITICAL *Must Do*

Figure 7

Aspirational (Optional): An aspirational problem or opportunity is optional because there's much less at stake. It's something they may get to someday, if possible. There's certainly nothing compelling or urgent here.

Critical (Serious): Critical problems need fixing, and prospects/clients often view them as urgent. There's usually a big and obvious cost for not solving the problem or a huge missed opportunity. An example of a critical, serious, or urgent problem could be filing a complicated tax return. The problem must be solved, and there's a hard-and-fast deadline. With critical problems, the prospect is probably feeling anxious and may be on the verge of emotional pain. If a prospect or client says, "We simply must get this taken care of," all you usually need to do is show them that you're the one who can "take care" of the problem.

You can see in Figure 7 that when a problem or issue—or even a desire—is both blatant and critical, you're in the quadrant where action takes place, resources are dedicated, and decisions are made to move forward.

Skok says that in business-to-business markets, you want to address problems that are blatant and critical because they are far more acute than those that are latent and aspirational. Blatant and critical problems interfere with business, putting careers and reputations at risk. I think you'll agree that the same dynamic applies in a business-to-consumer scenario.

Move Aspirational to Critical

With all of this said, if you are knowledgeable about your product/service, if you understand the significance of the problem, and if you know your prospect's context well, you might be able to move a problem from one quadrant to another rather quickly. You can do this in two ways:

1. Uncovering the problem that often underlies the aspiration
2. Discussing the implications or impact of not fixing the problem

As you help prospects get in touch with the impact of an unrealized aspiration or unresolved problem, what they originally perceived as aspirational can turn to critical.

Questions you might use to accomplish this include:

- How much is this situation costing?
- What is the cost of doing nothing?
- How does this affect you in the eyes of others?
- Tell me more about how this issue shows up on a regular basis.
- How is this impacting your client relationships?
- How long have you wanted to do this?
- How much does this frustrate you?
- What needs to be in place for you to act on this?
- How badly do you want to make this problem go away?

As you discuss a prospect's situation and discover various problems and opportunities, I advise that you determine the quadrant for each. Is the problem or opportunity blatant, critical, time-sensitive, and causing frustration? Jackpot! You're where you want to be.

None of the above? All is not lost; you just have some quality probing and teaching ahead of you.

RADICALLY RELEVANT ACTION STEPS

1. Take stock of the problems you profess to solve for prospects and clients. Where do they fall in this model? If they are not blatant and critical, what questions can you ask to amplify awareness, importance, and urgency?
2. Be transparent with your prospects. "This is not a critical problem. We can address this later. That, however, is something you need to fix as soon as possible."
3. Can you reposition your business and/or your messaging in a way that shows the critical nature of your work more quickly? And if so, how?

"Asking great questions will make you more money than merely answering questions."

—Bill Cates

RADICAL RULE OF RELEVANCE #15

Your prospects and clients aren't mind readers.

Never assume a prospect or client can read your mind and take the action you desire. If you want them to do something, ask them to do it. Use a call to action.

CHAPTER 21

Putting It All Together

Throughout this book, I've touched on principles of neuroscience and physics. I hope you've found these musings of a nonscientist helpful. To pull everything together, I'm going back to physics, and more specifically, to electrical engineering. The ensuing explanation may get me in trouble with my brother-in-law physicist, but what the heck. You'll get the point.

Think of how you communicate your value in terms of an electric motor, where two components are working together to create action—say, the crankshaft drive that turns the blade in a blender.

In an online article, Chris Woodward describes how an electric motor works: "The basic idea of an electric motor is really simple: You put electricity into it at one end and a shaft (metal rod) rotates at the other end giving you the power to drive a machine of some kind."

What's going on inside the motor? I don't know. Ask an electrical engineer or my brother-in-law.

Okay, you need more than a flippant remark? The electricity is pushed through a coil of wires and a series of magnets, creating a magnetic field. This field acts on the magnets on the shaft. This creates the force that gets the shaft to turn.

Ready to bring this metaphor home? Are you still with me, or are you checking your email? Come on back. Focus!

Think of the electricity that gets pushed into the motor as your *belief* in your full value proposition—all the ways you and your team provide value to your clients. Let's make the coil that surrounds the magnet the *relevant* part of your messaging. It's where you're communicating with prospects and clients in a way that resonates with them. The magnets (that attract and repel) can be the *compelling* part of your message—what you need to say that will move your prospects and clients to act on your recommendations.

In an electric motor, this activity is happening so fast that the shaft moves in an even motion. Voila! We have continuous movement.

Like the electricity flowing through the coil and magnets, so, too, must your messaging always be *relevant* and *compelling*. If one is missing, your business motor stops.

Knowledge is Not Power

One of my business mentors, Bill Wilks, taught me many things. The one lesson from Mr. Wilks (as I always referred to him) that has had the most impact on my business and personal life—is simple, yet profound: "Billy Cates, never forget this. Knowledge is important. Never ever stop learning. However, knowledge for knowledge's sake will not make you more successful. Only taking action on that knowledge will lead to more success."

With Mr. Wilks's message in mind, **what are you going to do differently as a result of reading this book?**

- Narrow your target market?
- Get crystal clear on your Right-Fit Clients?
- Communicate your differentiation in a way that creates value?
- Develop an effective Value Positioning Statement?

- Make your content marketing efforts more valuable and relevant?
- Tell your personal or company story in a way that demonstrates value?
- Move people to action with social proof and creating urgency?

I ended each chapter with Radically Relevant Action Steps. I recommend you go back to each chapter. Take a second look at those action steps. What can you implement right now? What can you implement over the next month or two? And what can you implement over the course of the next six to 12 months? Share these commitments to action with others so you gain clarity and are held accountable.

Make your actions relevant and compelling. Otherwise, you run the risk of being ignored and forgotten.

"Ideas will not make you more successful. Only action will."

—Mr. Bill Wilks

RADICAL RULE OF RELEVANCE #16

Test, test, test. This is a universal rule of marketing. You can make certain assumptions based on your own experience and/or intuition, and what other experts suggest, but you'll never know for certain until you test your ideas.

Wait! You're not done yet!

Be sure to take the *Radical Relevance Value Gap Assessment* in the Appendix that follows to see where you are and what might need some work. Consider having your entire leadership team take this assessment and compare notes.

I'm confident you will find this assessment a valuable investment in your time and attention. And as promised at the beginning of Part 1, I've included in the assessment examples how the MacKay CEO Forums has implemented what you've learned in this book.

RADICAL RULE OF RELEVANCE #17

Resist the urge to expand your target. The tendency for most is to widen their target to be more inclusive. Resist this. The more inclusive your messaging, the less impactful and effective it will be.

APPENDIX

The Radical Relevance Value Gap Assessment

Since the foundation of your business success consists of how you perceive, believe in, communicate, and deliver your value, it makes sense to assess your "Radical Relevance Value Gap"—the gap between where you are and where you want to be in your ability to attract and win more Right-Fit Clients.

The ultimate purpose of your messaging is to create action—to get prospects to want to know more about you, respond to your email or voice mail, schedule an appointment, work with you, and follow your recommendations. Anything short of creating action means missing the full potential of your message.

Whether you realize it or not, you and your team are constantly communicating your value. What you think, say, and write shows up in a myriad of places: emails to prospects, phone conversations, educational seminars, your website, your LinkedIn profile, networking events, and even social gatherings.

Your assessment begins in 3 seconds . . . 2 . . . 1 . . . go!

1. Have you taken stock of your complete value proposition by reviewing your entire client journey (prospect courtship, new client onboarding, ongoing client experience) to determine all the points where you provide value through the information you convey, things you teach, and questions you ask?

NO / SOMEWHAT / YES

(See Chapter 4)

MACKAY CEO FORUMS

MacKay has a very well-defined prospect-to-client journey that brings value quickly to prospective members. Prospects attend either a regular meeting as a guest or a breakfast where they receive immediate value. As they become members, in addition to the value from forum meetings, they get coaching from their certified forum chair and are provided with additional tools, such as the "MacKay Time Mastery Goal Setting Tool." In addition to regular meetings, members attend a two-day retreat and breakfast events, can listen to podcasts, and have access to many other tools over the course of membership.

2. Do you have a clear, well-defined target market(s) where you focus all or most of your marketing efforts and for which you have a clear, well-defined problem you solve?

NO / SOMEWHAT / YES

(See Chapter 6)

MACKAY CEO FORUMS

MacKay's well-defined target market consists of CEOs, executives, and business owners of privately held Canadian companies with revenue from $5 million to $500 million. Problems solved include how it's lonely at the top / lack of peers and a lack of time mastery.

3. Do you have a clear, well-articulated persona or ideal client profile(s) covering such things as demographic and psychographic attributes?

NO / SOMEWHAT / YES

(See Chapter 8)

MACKAY CEO FORUMS

MacKay's Right-Fit Clients (MacKay calls them best-fit members) are life-long learners, contributors, forward-thinking, and results-oriented. CEO Nancy MacKay begins phone calls with prospects describing a best-fit member. Within 30 to 60 seconds, both parties know if the fit is right or not. Because she cares about the forum group and company culture, she's looking to disqualify anyone who isn't a perfect fit.

4. Are you perfectly clear about the primary problem you solve for your Right-Fit Clients?

YES / NO

(See Chapter 7)

MACKAY CEO FORUMS

MacKay has identified the internal villain (the emotional problem) discussed in Chapter 7. CEOs resonate with the phrase, "It's lonely at the top." They also resonate with the lack of time mastery that the forums address head-on. The MacKay best-fit member wants to sell or grow their business, needs better balance in their life, or is new in their position and feeling overwhelmed.

5. When you talk about what makes you different (or distinct), do you always translate those attributes into clear benefits for your prospects and clients?

NO / SOMEWHAT / YES

Give it a try now. Take each point of distinction (feature), and tie it to a clear benefit.

(See Chapter 5)

MACKAY CEO FORUMS

1. MacKay CEO Forums provides the *least time-intensive* CEO peer-to-peer experience with only six meetings and a 2-day retreat each year. Because of the structure and processes used, members receive more value in less time.
2. MacKay CEO Forums provides the *highest impact* peer learning group because members can put an issue on the table every meeting, every time.
3. MacKay is the only CEO peer group in Canada with a chair certification program. Extensive training and certification ensures that the groups experience a consistently high level of expert facilitation and coaching.

6. Do you have a clearly defined process that you use to discover your prospects' and clients' problems before recommending any possible solutions?

NO / SOMEWHAT / YES

What are your discovery questions to get them to reveal their most important concerns?

(See Chapter 7)

MACKAY CEO FORUMS

MacKay uses an efficient process to discover problems the prospective member needs help solving. Knowing how busy CEOs tend to be, MacKay keeps their calls to 15 minutes. Once the prospect has been identified as a life-long learner, contributor, forward-thinking, and results-oriented, MacKay asks, "What issue or challenge would you like some help with from your peers?" The goal of the call is to get them to attend a regular forum or special breakfast meeting as a guest, where they can get help with their challenge.

7. Do you use a clear process to deliver value, solve your clients' problems, and/or take advantage of opportunities?

NO / SOMEWHAT / YES

If YES, does your process have a name that helps you further your differentiation in the market?

NO / YES

(See Chapters 4 and 20)

MACKAY CEO FORUMS

The forums are built for delivering value, solving problems, and maximizing opportunities. It's their reason for being. This work is done through regular meetings, retreats, summits, coaching sessions, and relationships developed with forum peers.

8. If someone were to ask, "What do you do?," do you have a clear, concise, and confident response?

NO / SOMEWHAT / YES

(See Chapter 10)

MACKAY CEO FORUMS

MacKay says: "Our dream is to populate the world with inspiring leaders. We offer peer learning groups for CEOs, executives, and business owners across Canada who are forward-thinking and action-oriented."

9. Have you developed your client-focused why? (Meaning, why you believe in the value of the work that you do.)

NO / SOMEWHAT / YES

(See Chapters 4 and 5)

MACKAY CEO FORUMS

MacKay believes that having inspiring leadership skills is the key to achieving success in all aspects of CEOs' lives. It is possible to achieve business success and not have to sacrifice health, family, and other goals. The company sees the impact its work has on people's lives.

10. Do you tell your prospects and clients about your client-focused why?

NO / SOMETIMES / YES

(See Chapters 4 and 5)

MACKAY CEO FORUMS

MacKay communicates its client-focused why in the first 15-minute phone call, at breakfast events, and at other events.

11. When you communicate your value through the written or spoken word, what is your goal? (Check all that apply—each is worth one point)

____ State my value simply so people understand what I do.
____ Attract the right prospects to my business.
____ Repel the wrong prospects for my business.
____ Move prospects to take action.

(See Chapters 4, 9 and 10)

MACKAY CEO FORUMS

MacKay checks all the items.

12. When you know you are a good fit for a prospective client, do you tell them that?

NO / SOMETIMES / YES

MACKAY CEO FORUMS

MacKay does this perfectly by reiterating the criteria for a best-fit member and the issues the prospect has said they'd like to examine with a peer group. "You are a best-fit member. Let's talk about finding the right group for you."

13. Have you articulated clearly defined company core values and created a culture that reflects those values both internally and externally? (Examples: "We value life-long learning." "We value open communication on our team; no hidden agendas." "We will always act in our clients' best interests first.")

NO / SOMEWHAT / YES

(See report in the Radical Relevance Toolkit)

MACKAY CEO FORUMS

MacKay's values are inspiration, confidentiality, accountability, service, and excellence.

MacKay is a B Corp (*www.BCorporation.net*) because it wants to be the best for the world, as well as the best in the world at offering peer learning groups. The company educates members on what a B Corp is and encourages them to become one.

14. Does your business have a clear mission statement that articulates a client-focused reason for being in business?

NO / SOMEWHAT / YES

(See report in the Radical Relevance Toolkit)

MACKAY CEO FORUMS

MacKay's mission is the same as its client-focused why. This is proper alignment. "Our dream is to populate the world with inspiring leaders."

15. Does your business have a clear vision for what you'd like to accomplish within the next three, five, or seven years?

NO / SOMEWHAT / YES

(See report in the Radical Relevance Toolkit)

MACKAY CEO FORUMS

Here's MacKay's: "Our vision is to double our impact in 3 to 5 years by growing to 2,000 members across Canada served by 120 forum chairs." The company is now working on a more global vision.

Calculate Your Relevance Gap Score

NO = 0 points

SOMEWHAT / SOMETIMES = 1 point

YES = 2 points

Question 12 = 1 point for each item you checked.

Maximum score = 32

A score of 0 to 16 = Yikes! Get to work now to stay in business!

A score of 17 to 24 = You are clearly headed in the right direction.

A score of 25 to 32 = Congratulations! You get it! Now, keep fine-tuning.

When your score is high, you are equipped with the knowledge and perspective to close the value gap and be far more relevant and compelling to your prospects and clients. Isn't that what you want?

ACKNOWLEDGMENTS

Anything Worth Doing is Rarely Done Alone

Shout outs go to:

Leo Pusateri for his introduction to this topic many years ago and his dedication to serving his clients with his Value Ladder.

To my information marketers summit colleagues, where the idea for this book came alive: Scott Cantrell, Dave Stelzl, Bill Whitley, Nelson Griswold, and Bart Camarota.

To my science advisory board: Lee Bristol, Scott Halford, Dr. John Molidor, and Dr. Lynda Shaw.

To my key staff members: Terri Frederick, Jennifer Shreve, and Jennifer Kreitzer. And to my daughter, Jenna Cates, for her invaluable research.

To a group of entrepreneurs who have been supporting each other for years: Willie Jolley, Suzi Pomerantz, Steven Gaffney, Zemira Jones, and Marissa Levin.

To my beta review team: Nancy MacKay, Dean Thibault, Ryan Wedel, Bruce Davison, Machen McDonald, Crystal Thies, William Wright, and Michael Schmidtmann.

To friends and colleagues who have supported and advised me on this and/or other projects: John Hurley, Les Picker, Joel Rosenberg, Randy Richie, Jay Magenheim, Maribeth Kuzmeski, Brian Moran, Chris Johnson, Al Fox, Erin Gay, Todd McDonald, Craig Strent, and Phil Jones. And so many others, too numerous to name.

A special shout out to Sandra Beckwith, my editor, who turned a long, sometimes rambling manuscript into a tight book that—I hope—will bring value to those who read it.

INDEX

REGISTER THIS BOOK FOR FREE RESOURCES

Get Instant Access to the Radical Relevance Toolkit*

When you go to www.RadicalRelevanceToolkit.com, you'll find a treasure trove of resources—all designed to help you acquire more Right-Fit Clients™.

Here's a sample of the resources you'll find:

- The Radical Relevance Action Guide
- Creating Your Radically Relevant and Compelling Website
- Creating Your Right-Fit Client™ Personas
- Your Relevant and Compelling Email Messaging Guide
- Creating Your Magnetic LinkedIn Profile

* We add new resources continuously. As a registered owner of this book, you will receive occasional updates alerting you we've added new tools to help you grow your business.

To register, go to: www.RadicalRelevanceToolkit.com

FREE RESOURCES FROM BILL CATES

Keep the Learning Going—Keep Your Business Growing

E-guides, Sample Scripts, Videos, and More

www.ReferralCoach.com/resources

WHEN YOU'RE READY TO MAXIMIZE RESULTS

Make a Small Investment in Your Business That Pays Big Dividends

The Cates Academy for Relationship Marketing

www.TheCatesAcademy.com